Robert Rabbin

INVISIBLE LEADERSHIP

Igniting the Soul at Work

AWAKENING

Acropolis Books, Publisher

LAKEWOOD, COLORADO • AUSTELL, GEORGIA

INVISIBLE LEADERSHIP
Igniting the Soul at Work

Published by Acropolis Books, Inc.
under its Awakening imprint

Acropolis Books, Inc.
Lakewood, Colorado
http://www.acropolisbooks.com

Cover design by Paige Bentzen, Remington Design
Interior design by Troy Scott Parker, Cimarron Design

Library of Congress Cataloging-in-Publication Data

Rabbin, Robert.
    Invisible leadership : igniting the soul at work / Robert Rabbin.
        p.   cm.
    Includes bibliographical references.
    ISBN 1-889051-35-7 (pbk.)

        1. Leadership—Religious aspects. 2. Work—religious aspects.
    3. Mysticism. I. Title

    BL626.38.R33 1998
    291.6'1—DC21   98-24772
                                                        CIP

Printed in the United States of America
This book is printed on acid free paper that meets standard Z 39.48 of the
American National Standards Institute.

∞

Credits

GRATEFUL ACKNOWLEDGEMENT is made for permission to use copyrighted material:

Forsyth, Karl, "Television Robs Our Children of Their Potential," Computers in Education web site (http://www.corecom.net/~karlfpp/asd-comp.htm).

Hanh, Thich Nhat, *Being Peace,* Parallax Press, Berkeley, CA, 1987.

Havel, Václav, "The Need for Transcendence in the Postmodern World," Independence Hall, Philadelphia, PA, 1994, Václav Havel web site (http://www.hrad.cz/president/Havel/speeches/index_uk.html).

Macy, Joanna, "The Great Turning," *Connections Magazine,* Sausalito, CA, Issue 3, February 1998.

Mitchell, Jennifer D., "Editorial: The Tigers," *World•Watch,* Washington, D.C., Vol. 11, No. 1, January/February 1998.

Power, Richard (ed.), *Great Song: The Life and Teachings of Joe Miller,* Maypop, Athens, GA, 1993.

Renesch, John (pub.), *The New Leaders,* Sterling & Stone, San Francisco, Spring 1994.

Robbins, Tom, "The Meaning of Life," Special Supplement Insert, *Life Magazine,* Vol. 14, No. 16, December 1991.

Toms, Michael, "Money & Spirit: An Interview with Jacob Needleman," Program #2241, New Dimensions Radio, 1994.

Trent, Barbara (director), Barbara Trent, Joanne Doroshow, Nico Panigutti, and David Kasper (producers), *The Panama Deception,* Empowerment Project Production, 1992.

For

Deborah Masters, dear friend;
Ram Dass, a trailblazer extraordinaire;
Allen Ginsberg, a ferocious truth-teller;
Muhammad Ali, whose conscience rocked the national boat;
Dr. Martin Luther King, whose courage is still an unclimbed
peak.

Appreciation

to John Renesch, for his friendship, support, and kind
foreword; to Anita Roddick, Martin Rutte, Jeffrey Mishlove,
Rolf Österberg, Perry Pascarella, and William E. Halal for
their comments; and to the staff and editors of Acropolis
Books.

Contents

Foreword

WHEN I WAS ASKED to write a foreword for Rob Rabbin's
new book I felt profound gratitude—a feeling that I expect
will linger for some time to come. I am grateful for being
associated with anything involving this man—a valued friend
and an admired colleague. I am also glad to add emphasis to
his words for he writes as he speaks, with truth and directness that can be matched by few other writers.

As an editor and publisher, I have worked closely with
over three hundred writers, many of whom have written
bestsellers. Yet I still find Rob's refreshing directness unique.
He is unwilling to be tentative or compromise himself to be
politically correct. He ignores the fluff and gets to the heart
of true leadership, true essence and true consciousness.

A word that could be used to describe his writing is
"radical." Why radical? Because Rob's words call for extreme
behavior and revolutionary thinking. But his writings sound
so commonsensical, you say. What he says strikes a chord
deep within you, you say. After all, who would debate the
value of self-actualization? Who would argue against maxi-
mizing awareness and personal authenticity?

There is a big difference between liking the poetry and
living the poem. Rob's words may feel good and make good

sense but they also call one forward to action. They challenge one to go beyond philosophical agreement and to integrate mystical thinking in one's everyday life and job. He directly addresses the incongruence which lies at the heart of so much of the cynicism that reigns supreme these days in the industrialized world.

This incongruence is the essence of human co-optedness, where we claim to hold certain values but we live our lives and work at our jobs under different rules of engagement. Rob's writing calls for engagement at the level of truth. This is why Rob's ideas may seem radical or extreme. He calls for a waking up—not just our minds but our entire selves. He calls for an end to the foolhardiness, the delusion and the insanity out of which we operate—to stop marginalizing the ideas verbalized by mystics through the ages. He calls for the legitimization of mystical understanding and actions that such understanding generates. It's time to stop tolerating leadership that originates from any less a place than an enlightened soul.

Recently, I received a review copy of a new book on leadership from a major publisher. This book will probably do quite well in the business marketplace. As I looked it over, I felt I was holding an antique—a collection of outmoded ideas which have been stated over and over again for the past dozen or so years.

Are the readers among the executive ranks so eager for ideas that they will consume re-packaged concepts? Why do so many authors and publishers conspire with their reading audiences in generating so much recycled garbage about leadership? Has the average business reader become like the mystery novel junkie who continues to buy the latest book by a favorite writer despite the fact that all plots are all basically the same?

We all know plenty about what kind of leadership is needed and the type of individual who is being called for by the challenges of these times. Dozens of books have been written about it, including a few of mine. Why then, do we continue to consume and digest text that discloses yet another technique, or the "ten ways to," or "how to see if you are…" or all the rest of the rubbish that ambitious consultants and profit-focused publishers continue to promote to the business community?

These times call for a kind of leadership never before required. All the old cliches are useless. In fact, most of the present criteria for leadership are more than outdated—they are outright dangerous if humanity is going to successfully transition to a new planetary consciousness. Now, what kind of leadership do we need?

If we are to successfully transition to a new planetary consciousness and transcend the global ecological crisis, the unemployment problem, the growing tension between the "haves" and the "have nots," and all the other concerns facing us as a species, we need to be more conscious. As Einstein stated years ago, we can't solve our problems thinking the same way we did when we created them.

New thinking doesn't mean thinking new thoughts. It means thinking differently. That may be difficult to grasp, but Rob makes it easier. Difficult or not, the human species is in the midst of entering a new era, an age of consciousness where reality as we have known it will no longer exist.

Leaders of the future are men and women who are keenly aware of the larger context of life. They are not merely focused on content or form—such as technique, procedure, methodology, shape, or application. These mostly fall into the physical or material plane of reality. These new leaders appreciate the value of the non-physical and non-material aspects of reality, heretofore unexplored by most business people. These folks recognize the value of context—source, intentionality, integrity, vision, values, and its larger purposes.

These are the concerns that mystics talk and write about. Able to appreciate context, these leaders are sensitive beyond what they see and hear. They have a keen sense that allows them to discern beyond the physical senses. They can pick up on "texture of the space," for instance knowing something or someone isn't right without any rational reason. In this way, they are irrational. They are deeply intuitive and can instantly pick up when the texture changes, the way a dog senses an earthquake before it occurs.

These leaders possess a strong knowing that goes beyond mental capacity; this knowing relies on their deep sense of interconnection with others, an appreciation for what philosopher Martin Buber called the "between."

If it sounds crazy and off-the-edge you might look at your own attachment to the status quo and your own appetite for rehashed enlightenment from the latest leadership guru wanting to build a reputation by identifying the "five key qualities," the way to lead, etc. We all have attachments to the way things are. They show up differently in each of us, but we all resist change. That's what makes real transformation so difficult.

This book provides its reader with anything that could possibly be needed to change the world, making real transformation easier. It provides the means to enhance awareness, to jolt consciousness so you can begin living and working in a way that makes sense in a nonsensical world. Rob can't make you do what you don't want to. No book can. But this one does hand over the key, leaving you with the key in hand, knowing all you need to do is use it to open the way toward a whole new future.

— JOHN E. RENESCH

Former publisher/editor, *The New Leaders.*
Editor, *New Traditions in Business, Learning Organizations,*
Leadership in a New Era.

Preamble

Our purpose is to consciously, deliberately evolve toward a wiser, more liberated and luminous state of being; to return to Eden, make friends with the snake, and set up our computers among the wild apple trees. Deep down, all of us are probably aware that some kind of mystical evolution is our true task. Yet we suppress the notion with considerable force because to admit it is to admit that most of our political gyrations, religious dogmas, social ambitions and financial ploys are not merely counterproductive but trivial. Our mission is to jettison those pointless preoccupations and take on once again the primordial cargo of inexhaustible ecstasy.

— TOM ROBBINS

Yes, the only real hope of people today is probably a renewal of our certainty that we are rooted in the Earth and, at the same time, in the cosmos. This awareness endows us with the capacity for self-transcendence. Politicians at international forums may reiterate a thousand times that the basis of the new world order must be universal respect for human rights, but it will mean nothing as long as this imperative does not derive from the respect of the miracle of Being, the miracle of the universe, the miracle of nature, the miracle of our own existence. Only someone who submits to the authority of the universal order and of creation, who values the right to be a part of it and a participant in it, can genuinely value himself and his neighbors, and thus honor their rights as well.

— VÁCLAV HAVEL

Preface

Searching for the invisible is not for the faint-hearted.
— STEPHEN HAWKING

THE PREFACE IS MY OPPORTUNITY to share with you some information about the scope and intention of this book. I would like to first speak about its content, or spine, and then its structure.

I recently watched film director Sydney Pollack being interviewed on a Bravo program called "The Actor's Studio." In telling the story of how he struggled to find the spine of the movie *Tootsie,* which he directed, he said it was crucial to know any movie's spine—its essence—which is to ask and answer several core questions: What is this movie really about? What is its meaning? What is the story it wants to tell, and what is the impact it wants to have? Once you have the movie's spine clear in your mind, you can move forward with a certain sense of assurance, relating everything to the spine. It's like knowing the size of your suit jacket, a 44 short. It makes shopping for words and anecdotes a lot easier.

I think this book has two spines: one is the true spine, and one is the false spine. The problem is that the true spine cannot be said. I don't mean it's a secret, or that I don't want to tell you; it literally cannot be said. No one—not poet, artist, saint, sage, shaman, mystic, philosopher, psychic, no one—no one has ever been able to speak about the true spine of this book: it is about an experience which defies description and explanation. With a gun to my head, I would say the true spine of this book is silence, though even that flawless word misspeaks and only orbits the truth—it doesn't land solidly.

With this dilemma standing before me as the first hurdle, I had to invent a second spine, a false one. It's false because I can say it, and I know that what this book is really about cannot be said. At some point we may be ready for the true spine, we may find ourselves ready to make the silence summit push, ready and willing to sacrifice our lungs and brains for some unspeakable glory of being.

Using the false spine as my guide, I would say this book is about awareness, reality, and leadership. It is about mysticism—the direct experience of reality—as leadership and leadership as mysticism. I want to completely redefine the word leader to imply a person's attainments in the realm of consciousness; henceforth, friendship with reality is prerequisite for leadership. Leader and mystic: they are now synonymous. When I use the word mystic and mysticism, I am not referring to organized religions and their doctrines, which I tend to think of as being political, not spiritual. I am referring to reality, and to knowers of reality. A mystic is a person who has direct and immediate experience of reality. A mystic's knowledge is not based on religious ideologies, creeds, or beliefs; rather, it trails direct experience like a meteor's fiery tail.

Though spirituality and mysticism are gaining some acceptance in our culture, our society as a whole is still suspect
of spirituality, and tends to marginalize mystics as the fringe
element of the spiritual set. We have forgotten that every
religion was founded by a mystic, and that the heart of the
world's spiritual traditions is the mystical experience. While
we may allow the words of long-dead mystics to console and
uplift our spirits and broken souls, we are not very inclined
to allow their radical views to mold the ways and means of
our commerce and social conduct. We seem to believe that
their visions and words are not practical enough to guide and
sustain us in our mundane pursuits.

If real life mystics happen to enter today's marketplace,
we don't allow their views to inform and shape our decision
making in the "real" world of business and government and
education; we certainly wouldn't trust a mystic in the role of
a general or admiral, or as head of Exxon. Mystics just cannot
produce results in the material world; they don't understand
how the world works. It's best if mystics stay in the ghettos
of spirituality, where we can visit if and when we want. This
is the common wisdom, which is not wisdom at all, but pure
foolishness.

Part of this misperception about the competency of
mystics is due to the nature of the mystic's path. As mystics
are weaned by meditation and silence from their addiction
to materialism, they naturally lose interest in the physical,
visible world in order to more fully explore and appreciate
the truer and more encompassing immaterial, invisible
world, the world of spirit. This is analogous to a medical
intern forsaking, for a time, all life except for the life within

the confines of a hospital. It is analogous to anyone who wants to achieve greatness and proficiency in an art or science: there is a time when they must devote themselves single-mindedly and exclusively to their chosen field. I'm sure that Baryshnikov, when he was young, didn't just take a couple of dance lessons. Mystics intern in reality, and study consciousness and awareness. Until they reach a level of maturity, they may not retain a strong relationship to the physical, visible world, mistakenly called the "real" world. However, when mystics achieve a certain level of maturity, of proficiency in their art, they may be returned by silence to this physical world with a clarity of vision and a dexterity of action that could never be matched by anyone who has lived exclusively in the visible world. Some of these mystics are beginning to be seen and heard on the national stage, outside the ghettoes of spirituality.

The prevailing conventional view that mysticism is disconnected from the real world is dead wrong. It is an unfortunate hallucination. The premise of this book is that unless and until people embark on a mystical path of knowledge, they are delusional, and represent a real and present danger to themselves and to others. The central truth of this book is that if we are not actively and vigorously exploring and expanding our consciousness, our awareness, then we are not qualified for leadership of any kind. At this time, with so much on the line, we simply must have leaders who can end madness by the sheer power of their clarity of cause and effect, their empathy towards reality, and their resoluteness to live and work as servants of life itself.

I am proposing that from now on, we—as a people, as a culture—allow and accept only mystics—mature mystics, mystics who hold in one hand the invisible world and in the other hand the visible—to have decision making authority in our society. These leaders will be an entirely new species of leader, who will serve us by serving the creative power of the universe, the mystic oneness from which all life comes. Their role—their job definition—is to know this power, to align with this power, to be taken and finally merge with this power. These leaders, these mature and maturing mystics, do not live in ashrams and convents, in monasteries and on mountaintops. They live here, where you live; they work right here where you work. They stand squarely on asphalt and astroturf; in bowling alleys and shopping malls and air-ports and boardrooms, with cell phones and pagers. These leaders drive in the carpool lanes every morning at 6:00 a.m. in Chevrolets and BMWs and 4×4s. But they are driving like whales in an ocean of clarity, setting everything in order by serving reality; whereas the old species of leader created through ignorance the very problems they were then chal-lenged to solve.

Our society is reality challenged, and this handicap has created problems, sadness, and suffering. We are *koyaanisqatsi*, a Hopi word which means crazy life, life in turmoil, life dis-integrating, life out of balance: a state of life that calls for another way of living. Our society is koyaanisqatsi. You know it and I know it.

We can correct the imbalance through a radical shift in our consciousness. We do not lack money or know how, time or resources. We lack only awareness, and even this we do not lack, but only forget to use. We'll have to get to work and refurbish our awareness with paint, furniture, and light fixtures made of reality, throwing out everything that is made of egoistic delusions. I am suggesting that we need to see the world as our painting, and that we begin to paint with a mystic's eye, with a lover's brush, and a palette of colors shocking to the conventional mind. We need a revolution of consciousness.

The mystics' canvas is a transcendent one, painted in the time beyond timelessness, where truth can never be spoken but is as real as concrete, finch, fire truck, and sea urchins basking in the early morning tidepools. The mystics' art transcends the pettiness and misperceptions of doctrines and beliefs; the mystics' art depicts our world and other worlds, our bodies and interstellar space, boardrooms and lucid dreams, glaciers and insects. The mystics' artful eye is opened wide and beholds the love-pulse within all living creatures; the mystics paint this in sudden downpours of color and intuition, of insight and primal sounds. Mystics square-dance with supernovas on Friday nights. They live as the servants of life's love-pulse and so serve happily and humbly each living thing. Their only purpose is to know and serve reality, to ignite the spiritual passion and intensity of all whom they meet.

––––––––––

The horizontal line above is part of this book's structure. It is the equivalent of a scoop of sorbet, which is served in fine restaurants between courses to cleanse the palate. This line is a scoop of silence, a pause in which you may refresh yourself by shifting attention from these words to your inner awareness, or your breath. Give yourself a chance to get behind my words.

The truest meaning in poetry is found behind and beyond the poem, in the reverberations of sound that carry all the way to silent meaning. There the soul is most deeply touched by the same source, the same artistic inspiration, that touched the poet. Poems are bridges to a world of heightened beauty, meaning, and significance. Entering this world, our soul ignites with recognition, our flailing minds stop and tilt—and in that tilt of our usual mind the spectacular order and intelligence of reality emerges. Awakening to reality is to step out of time, even for a splinter of a second, but in so doing we are met by eternity, tutored, and returned home to time, family, and friends. I think the best poetry evokes our soul; it doesn't explain anything.

I would like to evoke, not explain. I want be wild as I write; I don't want to be tame. I don't want to homogenize what I have to say. I don't care to be pedantic. I want to push out into a wild sea and risk disaster for the sake of that which is beyond the mind and intellect. I am after bigger fish than comprehension, agreement or disagreement. I am not aiming to comfort anyone, but to disturb in the extreme. I hear Kabir shout in my left ear, "Those who hope to be reasonable about it fail. The arrogance of reason has separated us from that love."

I am not interested in appealing to anyone's rational mind, to inform or persuade, but to evoke their wild heart of ecstatic love.

Much will be asked of leaders in the coming years. They will be expected to help us redress an array of social problems, to help us cure illness and end epidemics, feed the hungry, end brutality and war, stop the displacement of indigenous tribes, reverse the pollution and degradation of the environment, curtail corruption and greed, safely dispose of industrial and nuclear waste, educate children without crushing their free and spiritual minds. These problems are solvable by us—all of us, together, each contributing in a unique way—if we sincerely want to and if we will use the preeminent power of our inherent transcendent awareness.

I believe that awareness is more useful and practical than intellectual strategies and models and principles and answers and prescriptions: I believe that our own dormant powers of consciousness can reveal instantly what we must do and how we must do it. To explore our consciousness and expand our awareness of reality is to climb high enough to see the whole landscape of cause and effect. We have betrayed ourselves by turning from consciousness; we have become entranced by the visible world and have forgotten its invisible origin. We have fallen in love with the chicanery of our mind and forgotten the profound counsel of our soul. We have become belligerent towards nature and our carelessness is starting to pile up like stinking garbage. We are willing to do almost anything for money, and we are silent witnesses to the desecration of entire populations. I know this is not the whole story, but it is a part of the story that is important to consider in light of our capacity for mystical knowledge. We need to get our heads screwed on right.

We need to discover our own inner capacity for mystical knowledge to bring balance and sanity to an otherwise koyaanisqatsi life. In this alliance with reality, each of us will be able to apply unprecedented invention and wisdom to those dis-eases of our lives; we will become gift and grace bestowing behemoths; we will restore the lost paradise for ourselves, to each other and the entire living Earth, and future generations will revere us for our great effort and work.

This book is my contribution to the public discourse about who we are and where we are going and how we are going to get there. I believe in the power of consciousness and the awakened soul. I believe that we are all linked to the mystical source of creation, and waking up to that is not as difficult as it may seem. I believe that we'll be fine if we simply drive our tent poles deep into the earth of that essential ground and stay put. After that, let whatever comes, come. Let whatever is to happen, happen. We'll be ready.

Once we are standing knee deep in the radiant earth of our soul, I trust, absolutely and beyond any doubt, in our collective spirit and ingenuity to create new values; and from those new values, new priorities and commitments; and from those, new systems and structures and institutions. I know that we can transform fear into freedom, hatred into love, violence into peace, poverty into abundance, pollution into purity, and separation into connection.

We have only this one thing to do, only this one thing: show the face of who we truly are, that we and others may see the brilliance of that true face and know its redemptive love and wisdom. If we want to know how to do this, how to find and show the brilliant face of our inner truth, the answer is this: want to. We must simply want this more than anything else. That is all. Put nothing else in front of this one desire, and your face will burst like a thousand suns upon this newly-happy Earth.

It is my hope that something in this book—a word, a phrase, a story—will cause your world to stop, your mind to tilt, and your soul to ignite in silence. I believe that the soul, fully aroused and on fire, irreversibly awake, is the greatest power in the world. If we can hear our soul's silence as loudly as the silence of the high desert at night, then we will know exactly how to bring ourselves and the world of our making into accord with reality, and we will do it with wisdom and love.

Genesis

In the following pages I offer nothing more than simple facts, plain arguments, and common sense; and have no other preliminaries to settle with the reader than that he will divest himself of prejudice and prepossession...and generously enlarge his views beyond the present day.

      – THOMAS PAINE

THE GENESIS OF THIS BOOK was a week-long vision quest I went on about ten years ago down in Mexico. I slept in a small hotel in a fishing village whose name I've forgotten. The quest wasn't very traditional; it was self-styled—home-made, not store-bought—one of many I've invented for myself and others over the years. During the day, I would walk the beach, sitting down from time to time to stare at the horizon with one set of eyes and, with another set, to follow my breath to its lair. In the evening, I would drink beer and eat grilled shrimp, reflecting on the day's meditations.

I went on this trip to meditate and reflect on my work. Something was out of kilter with either the *what* or the *how* of my work life. I was leaking life force, which is to say that I was becoming spiritually depressed.

At that time, I was a consultant whose clients were mainly senior executives in small to mid-sized corporations. My role as a "clarity coach" was to enhance my clients' awareness of themselves and their relationships. As a function of my own years of training in mindfulness, I could usually see and point out some crucial aspect of a relationship or situation that no one else could see, and these insights would then empower my clients to realize their goals and purposes. I enjoyed my work and my clients were pleased with my contributions. Still, I felt somehow compromised: a malaise of sadness had entered my true heart.

My true heart had developed during the decade previous to my consulting career when I studied spiritual science with a meditation master. During most of those years, including four in India, I was shaken by personal earthquakes of inner awakening. I had discovered exotic and profound worlds within myself and, as a consequence, experienced a steady reshaping of the view of reality bequeathed to me by various authorities as I was growing up. My true heart was in this continuous exploration of inner consciousness and its expression in the world.

I suspected that in supporting my clients' efforts, I was somehow neglecting the core of my true heart, which had been aroused and forged in those earthquakes. I may have taken on too much of my clients' reality in order to be of service to them. My clients were primarily interested in business success; I was primarily interested in the silent depths of inner revelation. I felt that I wasn't breathing the air I was meant to breathe and was slowly suffocating. The vivid light of creation was dimming. So, I did what I always do when I feel blocked, conflicted, or out of alignment: I went inward.

Going inward through meditation and self-inquiry is a superior adventure: one never knows what one will find or the degree to which what is found will impact or transform one's life. Perhaps some will wonder at this "going inward" as an appropriate solution to life's conflicts and dilemmas. For me, it is in all cases the first and most important thing to do: the silence I find at my center is the voice of my soul, and that is what I listen to and follow. I usually augment what I hear in silence, later, with my intellect—to analyze, plan, coordinate and so on—but I must receive the first impulse, the primal vision, from the indwelling silence.

On the fourth day, the voice of silence spoke wordlessly and unequivocally: *Teach the mysticism you know to leaders.* My initial reaction was terror. *No way!* I didn't want to do this. This was over ten years ago, when words like *spirit* and *soul* had barely found their way into the business lexicon. I also felt that, in spite of almost 20 years of spiritual practice and study, I knew less than when I began and was losing more ground every day. I felt this would be a nut too hard to crack, and I would die of ridicule and starvation. I said so.

Do it said the voice, *and you will be guided. It is your path.*

I remember drinking a dozen or so beers that night. The following day, I went back to the beach. I sat silently and waited for a confirming conversation, which was not long in coming. *Teach the essence of hamsa to world leaders. Don't worry.*

I protested. *Hamsa?* Why not just put a gun to my head and pull the trigger. Hamsa is a Sanskrit word which means

"supreme transcendent wisdom." Hamsa is a mantra that sig-
nifies our unity with that consciousness which pervades every
atom of this universe and connects all living beings. I was
supposed to talk to leaders about *this?* It's one thing to talk
about mysticism and consciousness and meditation with like-
minded people; hell, I had lived in one spiritual ghetto or
another for almost twenty years. I could certainly talk that
talk. But in corporate boardrooms? With senators and presidents, with moguls and magnates? With *Ross Perot?*

I drank many beers that night, and chased each one with
a tequila shot—or was it the other way around?—trying to
come to grips with this "vision." I knew that resistance was
out of the question—what's the point of spending a lifetime
unearthing the voice box of that small, still voice if one is not
going to listen and follow? Still, I was terrified. I knew intuitively that this path would require me to encounter my every
fear, insecurity, doubt, pretense, and delusion.

It was one thing to be a consultant who drew privately on
spiritual practice and principles to help roll clients' wheels
along the path of their aspirations; it was another thing alto-
gether to stand for and speak about "unity with the cosmos."
I began to hyperventilate, afraid of things unseen and unknown. My spiritual teacher said, "To understand hamsa is to
experience our unity with the cosmos." Talk about an intimi-
dating mission statement.

Upon returning home to Mill Valley, California, I began to
convert the townhouse I was renting into a retreat center and
to tell friends and associates what I was up to. The ones who
didn't laugh looked at me carefully for a long time, trying to
see if it was me, or someone else. It didn't take a psychic to

know what they were thinking, *Hmmm, it must have been some bad fish, or maybe the water. He'll be okay in a few days.* Even those colleagues who shared my spiritual inclinations advised me against being so bold. *Better to say something that will get you in the front door, and then slowly reveal your real work. Better to advertise high performance team building, or visionary leadership, or something they can get their hands on and their minds around.* I remember having dinner with my best friend and his wife. *Are you fucking nuts? Nobody in business wants that.* Consider, this was ten years ago.

I didn't disagree with them. But I couldn't betray myself, either. I knew that avoidance would be far more painful than experiencing whatever fears and trepidations I had. I would just have to go in the direction that silence had pointed out. A dear friend of mine once said that if we never leap from the precipice of our fears and attachments, we'll never find out whether the soul-force of the universe might catch us.

Shortly after my return from Mexico, I had the first opportunity to publicly test my vision. I had agreed, before going to Mexico, to deliver a morning talk to the legal affairs department of a billion dollar pharmaceutical company. As I was unpacking my briefcase, the people began to file in: one three-piece grey suit after another. One or two wore break-set white vertical stripes, and they looked vaguely like gangsters from a 1930's movie.

The head of the department came over and asked for my card. Returning to his seat, he looked at my card, which by then had the word hamsa on it, and asked, "What the hell does hamsa mean?"

This is it, I thought. They're going to throw you out on your ass. I actually began putting my notes and pens and markers back in my briefcase. "Hamsa," I said, "means supreme, transcendent wisdom."

The attorney's face tensed and his head fell forward into his hands. He shook his head back and forth for a minute. I closed my briefcase and prepared to leave. He looked up.

"My God," he sighed, "do we ever need some of that around here."

The Big Bang

*I have no doctrine. I only point out something. I point out reality, I
point out something in reality which has not or too little been seen.*

— MARTIN BUBER

I WAS BORN IN 1950, and became a mystic eleven years later
when the hand that made this world reached into my bedroom and window shook me awake. I had been skiing with
my family at Sestrierre, near our home in Torino, Italy, when
I fell on the slopes and broke my left leg in three places. In a
cast up to my hip, I spent a month in bed. During that time,
I started leafing through the *World Book Encyclopedia*. I remember my amazement as I wandered through the worlds,
turning page after page. My mind was stretched and opened
wide, like a hungry mouth devouring a sumptuous buffet.
Reading about the universe and its origins and vastness was
a powerful initiation into mystery and awe. One day, I felt a
presence enter the room. I could feel it but not see it. Still,
my eyes widened. I became silent and attentive. Then I just
knew. Behind this visible world is an invisible presence, conscious and creative, the maker of all the worlds I'd been

reading about. This presence is God. I am this presence. So are you.

Mysticism refers to this presence, to the unfathomable mystery of creation. I know that tomes have been written on the subjects of God, mysticism, soul, mind, and reality, some of which require lifetimes of study. It is a vast field of study, with innumerable nuances of meaning and truth. There is much scholarly debate about the difference between a real mystical experience and a hallucination, or between the first level and third level mystical experience, or whether a vision of the blue pearl is higher than the green pearl, or if there are seven chakras or thirteen. Some people clamor for scientific proof of a mystic's experience.

I am not particularly fussy about scholarly precision. I am not interested in models of mysticism, or theories of spiritual evolution, or benchmarks of authenticity. The study of mysticism is very different from the experience of mysticism; to explain mysticism is very different from demonstrating it. Mysticism is a wild sea, which we just need to enter. I think that once we enter it, *it* won't let go of us, and then we'll continue to learn more and more. But let's just get our feet wet to begin with. Mysticism refers to a current that, once entered, takes us farther and farther out to sea, in its own time and in eccentric ways.

A mystic is simply a person who has experienced the heart of life, and who thus knows that an essence—love, truth, spirit, silence, Self, consciousness, Tao, God—exists every-where, uniting all into a geometry of relatedness. I believe that we are all mystics because we have all been deeply touched and moved by an epiphany or struck by splendor, by a sumptuous lightning flash that lifts body, mind, and heart into the soul of the world's creative power. In this collision with essence, we stretch ourselves from here and now to places and times both past and future; we become part of the endless inscrutability of life itself. Mystics see their life in that instant as a gift and function of a universal force of extreme consciousness, and in that same moment become drenched with clarity, love, wisdom, and compassion, the inescapable fragrances of the mystic's life. Seeing life in this way, one's mind and spirit become free, inventive, and generous; one sees oneself everywhere.

We live within a mystical nexus with life, with spirit, with God. A mystic is a person who *becomes* a human being by learning to live in this awareness through diligent work. Mystics work, practice, devote, and dedicate themselves to the great challenge of becoming who they already are. A mystic's path wends through the limitations of conditioning, through superstition and belief, the dark nests of troubling desires and fears, dependencies and attachments, false idols and mistaken identities. A mystic's path cuts right through delusion and ignorance towards reality's panoramic grandeur.

A mystic is not some special person endowed with super-human virtue or sanctity. A mystic is a person who con-sciously seeks significance in living. In seeking significance, *meaning,* mystics put their own personal borders and barri-cades at risk in the mystery, and invite awe, wonder, exhilara-tion, depth, silence, beauty, and love to overrun them. They are willing to be taken by the breath within the breath. They sleep on the exposed cliff face, looking down at Yosemite

Valley, high and vulnerable to the light of sudden beauty and revelation.

A person in love is a mystic. A person who disappears while watching a hawk's wings dip and slice the invisible currents is a mystic. A person holding an infant for the first time is a mystic. A person worshipping at the feet of redwoods or wading in glacial lakes is a mystic. In all these instances, and countless others, we notice there is a moment in which we leave ourselves and enter something larger. We become the beauty we behold; we lose ourselves as one, and then find ourselves in all. This is not an uncommon experience. This is the path of the mystic. This is the portal of reality: leaving the contours of the small self for the grand wilderness of love, of beauty, of unity.

In a very real and practical sense, are we not all mystics? Have we not all experienced such moments of beauty, harmony, and unifying love? We all know this moment, in which we are likely to say, "So this is how it is!" It isn't that these men and women to whom we turn for inspiration and guidance in the spiritual realm are a special class of people, possessing powers and insights unavailable to the rest of us. It is just that they tend not to forget these moments of surpassing and cleansing clarity. They go more deeply into what is revealed in these moments of oneness. They invite that oneness to play through them. Their experience of oneness becomes a constant stream that refreshes their whole being: with each breath, with each thought, they are carried by that current.

Mysticism is the art of the real, and mystics are people who seek to know the real. As we become acquainted with,

and then know, and then intimately love reality, an automatic
re-ordering of our values occurs; reality itself imparts this
order and this order unveils a banquet of sweet significance.
Our every impulse is a product manufactured by reality
itself. Our lives and our legacies are thus made beautiful as
we become the helpmates of reality.

However, mysticism has gotten a bum rap from popular
culture, which seems to have become entranced by the
unreal. Even the dictionaries are equivocal: they say that
mysticism is the "direct, immediate, intimate communion
with ultimate reality." Then, those same dictionaries state
that mysticism is "vague and groundless speculation" or
something "cryptic, unintelligible, and obscure." The resolution of this paradox is crucial, for if we—as individuals,
communities, and societies—are to relieve the tensions and
burdens and complex problems snarling at our heels, we had
better understand reality. "What is real?" is the single most
important question we can ask. We should not be afraid that
this inquiry into reality will lead us astray, that it will be
obscure and irrelevant.

The resolution of this paradox can be found in the same
dictionaries that present the paradox. Mysticism, reality, *is*
unintelligible, but only to the faculties of reason and intellect.
Reality is eminently perceptible and knowable, but we must
first travel deep into the uncontrollable wilderness of heart
and soul, of wonder and awe, of silence and being. To know
reality, we have to abandon our addiction to rational analysis
in favor of intuition and insight. We have to see ourselves and
our world with an innocence uncorrupted by the false cer-
tainties of our ideas and beliefs. We have to touch the actual

heat of reality with the same immediacy of feeling as placing our palm, open and facedown, on a glowing stovetop.

I don't know anyone who is not interested in the significance of what is ultimately real and meaningful and beautiful. Mysticism is the well from which we can draw the water of true values; it is where we learn of significance and meaning and where we learn to live in accord with and in service to universal truths, affirmed and ratified by mystics from every society and culture which has ever existed.

I am saddened at mysticism's bum rap, because it means that we have grown suspicious of what is real and meaningful. We have created a society whose de facto values and principles are starkly antithetical to mystical feelings. Wouldn't you like to change this, to legitimize conversations about mystical reality—about significance and love and silence and beauty and consciousness—in offices and meeting rooms and buildings throughout America and the world?

The Real World

Reality has no inside, outside, or middle part.

— B O D H I D H A R M A

OVER THE YEARS, I've had many close encounters of a spiritual kind. Some were very powerful and took me years to integrate. Some were pleasant, some beatific, some were terrifying. I have been transported out of time. I've stepped out of my body as from a pile of dirty clothes and drifted in light. Once, in meditation, I went to the center of the Earth and heard her breathe. I've been stopped dead in my tracks by an overwhelming feeling of love, my eyes misting over, heart crumbling, wanting to touch every single person, every living creature, with gratitude and tenderness. I've seen the light that is the life of all things, which comes from someplace… I don't know where. I have glided as in a sailplane over landscapes from other worlds. I have sat on God's front porch in my own backyard and felt the tremors of new creation. I've been demolished by a silence and peace, by an expansiveness, for which I have not a single word. These experiences

expanded my contact with the dimensions and facets of
reality and affected my perception of reality.

I used to lead a weekly class in Mill Valley. People would
come by and we'd meditate for a while, and then I'd usually
give a talk, followed by some lively dialogues with whoever
showed up. There was a core group of people who came
nearly every week, including one young woman who drove
up from San Jose, a three hour roundtrip. One of the regulars
would follow along for a while, sinking into her own silence
and breathing, happy to let go of herself and her ideas. But
then something in her would snap, and she would bark out,
"What does this have to do with reality?" She understood me
up to a point, and I understood her up to a point. To me,
what we were and are speaking about, a mystery of incomparable depths and dimensions, is reality. My friend's reality
was limited to what she could see and feel and control and
affect. She was always most interested in finding new strategies to get her way, to realize her ambitions, to get and to
have. She talked of mastering her life; I talked of serving life.
This is why I said earlier that we are reality challenged. Our
society has built a single lane road, one of materialism, which
we use to travel on through reality. No wonder there is so
much traffic and so many accidents!

The world that is perceptible to our senses and the world
of our concepts and beliefs is certainly a part of reality, but
it is so tiny as to barely be a blip on the screen. Unless what
is called the real world is put in the proper context and perspective, it is no more than a dream. A dream. A mystic
knows this. Spiritual experiences help us to loosen our grip
on the materialistic view of reality as the dominant one. They

help us to soften and expand the boundaries of who we think we are.

We must each find the connection with reality through our own investigation of self, mind, and reality. The following principles are not a definitive description or rule book of the mystic's universe of intuitive knowing, but represent a partial record of the insights I've gleaned from 30 years of mystical pursuits. I present them so you will know what I mean about the playing field of mysticism. Do not accept or reject what I have learned; neither response will be helpful. Rather, read with attention, and see if you can notice some quickening of recognition flicker within you. If you do, go there, go towards that flickering and quickening. That is the place of true learning for each of us.

1. Consciousness is the first cause of the universal mani-festation, a creative vibration whose echo is the manifest cosmos.

2. This creative consciousness is the animating life force of all living creatures, and it permeates every atom of the entire cosmos. Realizing this, our fundamental experi-ence of life shifts from dualistic to unitive, from doing to non-doing, from becoming to being.

3. We are, in our essence, overflowing with presence, intuition, and joy. *Overflowing with presence, intuition, and joy* is who we are. When we touch the true skin of our essential body, we feel this is so, without cause or con-dition or qualification.

4. Everything is sentient, all things are alive and conscious, regardless of how inanimate they seem to our gross eye. Everything is a vibration of the primal consciousness, apparent differences being differences of frequency.

5. All living things are related. If you touch *here,* you touch *there.* This is the root of the maxim "What goes around, comes around." The categorical distinctions we use to separate ourselves from others and the world are hallucinations, which prevent us from seeing that we are the world, and the world is us.

6. The individual self does not exist. It's not that we don't exist; we just don't exist as independent of everything else, and we don't exist solely within the package of our body/mind. This is a bit paradoxical. On the one hand, we feel that we are the story and history of our body/mind; on the other hand, we have all experienced how love, beauty, and joy exist only when we transcend that story. Our individuality is a barrier to the deepest and truest experience of being alive, in which we lose and forget ourselves.

7. We live in multiple dimensions and have access to powers, capabilities, and knowledge beyond the range of motion of our body, senses, and mind. Mystics may directly access the entire database of consciousness, and demonstrate massive intuition, clairvoyance, precognition, energetic healing, bilocation.

8. Every thought and action is a potent seed which bursts into the world, sooner or later. We cannot easily sort out the intricate and complex web of cause and consequence, seed and flower. Nonetheless, every rooster comes home to roost. If we kill, we should expect to be killed. If we degrade, pollute, and spoil, we should expect that, look for that. If we deprive others, we will soon be deprived. If we show kindness and generosity to others, watch it return. We live on a wheel and we turn that wheel with our thoughts and actions.

9. Life is eternal, the manifestations of life are impermanent. Everything exists in its own cycle of birth, growth, decay, and death. Everything, from a thought to a mayfly to a galaxy. With the subtle eye, we see that there is no solidity at all, there is only an incredible festival of energy. Solidity and duration are conventions of our perceptual faculties. *Now* is the truest expression of reality.

10. Attachment is suffering. Let everything go as quickly as it comes. All of our ideas, identities, thoughts, opinions, grudges, unresolved expressions, motives, wounds, angers, fears, hopes, dreams, loyalties—create the individual self, which is the barrier to experiencing the essential self.

11. The ideas of original sin and satan are fear- and shame-based hallucinations. They do not exist in any form whatsoever. We cannot return to Eden, for we have never left. We cannot betray God, for we are that God.

We can only forget that this is so, and that forgetting is
sin and punishment enough.

12. Thought and awareness are distinct forms of perception. Thinking is a limited form of perception and
cannot experience reality directly. Awareness is without
inherent limitation; awareness is the experience of
reality.

13. The mystical experience is a wild sea in which wave
upon wave of depth and significance crash over us;
layers, facets, and dimensions of the great mystery
open and befriend us. It is, as John Lee Hooker said,
"Yes! Yes! So sweet!"

The mysticism I know is simple: it is the silence that falls
upon us in a moment of beauty, of creation, of love, of communion, of deep reflection. The word mysticism has come,
colloquially, to represent the arcane, the abstract, the
remote, the mysterious; however, the exact opposite is true.
It means, literally, to experience an immediate connection
with life itself. As simple as it is, a lot can get in the way of
our experience of life. We have to be reminded, or awakened, or jolted into a recollection of the obvious and
self-evident simplicity mysticism implies.

Within each person is a depth of being that is silent, and
that silence embraces the entire universe: rock, salamander,
iris, and sun. The experience of silence is exquisite and so
different from our conventional mode of experience that it
can scarcely be spoken of, let alone taught as most things are

taught. There are many paths of and to silence. My path took me to the East, to India, where I studied with a meditation master. I learned that silence is, itself, the great teacher, the great explainer, the great illuminator. Silence is chronic and compulsive intuition and spontaneity. It is a light spring rain from a cloudless sky beyond the reach of the mind. That rain is spiritual nourishment to all living things, and all things are living.

Mysticism refers to the self-transcendent clarity that is found in silence, in love, in beauty, in the explosive aftermath of poetry and music, in the awesome *fact* of forests and mountains, in the revelry of lovemaking and carnivals of eroticism, in the rhythms of dance and the cadence of song, chant, and prayer. The mystic is in love with that which will not brook any formulation. It cannot be turned into principles and paradigms. It is too free, endlessly creative, and joyful for any of that.

The mystic language is not meant to inform, convince, or persuade; the words are as missiles meant to stop the mind with a judder, to collapse reason, time, and self. In the collapsed rubble, spontaneity lurks, and the silence-infested clarity of reality purrs purposelessly and gloriously.

The best I can do, by way of teaching what can't be taught, is to invoke silence. This silence is of utmost importance, much more so than anything I or anyone else can say. The mysticism I know, I can only point to: an exquisite silence within the deep core of each human being which can be directly experienced. This inner silence is itself the true seat of power and teacher of wisdom. I learn from this silence. I see from this silence. Silence opens the heart and clears the mind. I trust this silence to provide clarity, courage, and truth. This is what I trust, and this is what I know inheres in each person: a clear mind and an open heart. It is not enough to agree or disagree; in order to be authentic, the indwelling silent beauty must be realized by each one of us. Otherwise, we will be merely the stooges of gossip and rumor and reality by agreement.

The French film director Jean-Jacques Annaud, in describing his work, said, "I want my images to carry an emotion you can hardly describe with words. They ring a secret bell in your heart, and those are the bells I love to ring." The secret bell I love to ring is silence. It is my hope that something in this book will arouse your inner silence, and that this aroused silence will cause you to contemplate who you are, essentially; and to reflect upon what you are doing, how you are doing it, and why.

The essence of mysticism is really the essence of significance: it is a values-based approach to life in which the values are inspired by a direct and immediate experience of transcendent reality. To be a mystic is to belong to life itself and to live in its continuous eruption of silence and beauty; it is to be joined with life beneath the shells and surfaces of the visible, to swim in the invisible depths, to travel deep, deep into the subterranean caverns of suspended breath, to climb the exalted high peaks of snow-blind rapture, and finally to return to the porches of our homes where we sit contentedly with the ones we love, and in so loving, loving all. How is this obscure? How is this irrelevant?

Dear Mr. Balsekar

To penetrate into the essence of all being and significance, and to release the fragrance of that inner attainment for the guidance and benefit of others is the sole game which has any intrinsic and absolute worth. All other happenings, incidents and attainments can, in themselves, have no lasting importance.

— MEHER BABA

ABOUT EIGHT YEARS AGO, I got it into my head to interview a dozen or so spiritual teachers and gurus for a book about mysticism and business leadership. In retrospect, that book idea, which only got about four inches off the ground, may have been the precursor to this book.

I was going to ask each of the people on my list the same questions, all of which had to do with the true nature of self, mind, consciousness, and reality. My idea was to point these conversations towards business leaders, with the hope that their interest in spiritual inquiry and self-knowing would be aroused.

I heard that Mr. Ramesh S. Balsekar was coming to Mill Valley, where I lived, and would be holding a few *satsangs*—

meetings for the purpose of inquiring into truth—with students and other interested people. This was great news, as
Mr. Balsekar had been the translator of Nisargadatta Maharaj,
a well-known mystic who lived in Bombay and who had influenced many seekers with his unforgiving style of inquiry. In
addition to that, Mr. Balsekar had been an executive with the
Bank of India. I thought that he would be a perfect person
with whom to speak about mysticism and its relationship to
business.

I attended one of his satsangs, which was held in a private
home in Tiburon. Afterward, I made my request and he
agreed to meet me. The next day, I went back to the same
house, where he escorted me to the interview area. Two
chairs had been arranged on a small patio. A round table
with a glass top stood nearby, on which I put my tape
recorder. After a few introductory pleasantries, we began.

I explained the purpose of the book in greater detail than
I had the evening before. He listened intently, and then asked,
by way of summarizing, *So you want to write a book about meditation and self-inquiry and self-knowledge for the businessman, is
that correct?*

Yes, that is correct.

He asked why. His tone was direct and matter-of-fact.

For some reason, that question threw me. I had expected
him to be more sympathetic, I suppose. *What do you mean
why? Isn't it obvious?* I didn't say that, I just thought it. And
then I paused, not knowing what to say.

I had never really asked myself that question. I just
assumed everyone wanted to know the truth about themselves and about the world. I was nonplused. I came back

with, *Well, you were an executive with the Bank of India, and you also pursued self-knowledge with Nisargadatta. How did that pursuit affect your duties with the bank?*

Not at all, he said. It was only after his retirement that he began to get serious about self-inquiry. Then he veered away from the personal. He asked, *Why should business people read your book?*

To be encouraged to contemplate their own Self.

What will they get from doing that?

They will wake themselves up and experience their true nature.

How will that help them in their business?

I don't know.

Can you give them something concrete that they can use in their business?

No.

Can you promise them something, like Maharishi Mahesh Yogi? He promises that if you meditate for ten minutes a day you will lower stress and increase your energy, clarity, and productivity. Will people get this from reading your book?

Maybe, but that's not what I'm really offering. I'm offering conversations about truth.

A businessman is not interested in truth. A businessman is interested in profit. Is your book going to help him make a profit?

No.

Then why would he want to read it?

That was the end of our conversation, and the end of the book. I thought I ought to be able to answer him better than I did, which was not at all. His questions were good business

questions: who is your market, what need does your product
fill, how will you position it? Those question inevitably
become other questions of the same genus: Do you have a
business and marketing plan? Do you have sufficient capital-
ization? Do you have your start-up team? Corporation or
sole proprietor, public or private? Mr. Balsekar seemed to be
reminding me that the first, second, and third questions of a
business are related to how we make money. Later, I would
come to realize that the first, second, and third questions of
a business should be related to how we serve the welfare and
well-being of all living things.

After our conversation, I had to admit that my premise
may have been faulty. Business leaders *would* wonder at the
practicality of spiritual inquiry and discovery. Would a deeper
and clearer understanding of the human spirit, the nature of
mind, and the power of consciousness really have contact
points with the day-to-day demands and priorities of running
a business? Is the subtle realm of spiritual insight useful and
relevant in a business context?

—————

I love questions. The first word I ever said was "why." That
predisposition was the cause of much subsequent drama in
my life. I could never accept anything when I was younger. I
kept saying that word, *why.* Why? It was a current that pulled
me out into deep waters, a siren song to great adventures
and near disasters. While my older brother went off to law
school, I went off to run with the bulls in Pamplona and then
to Finnish Lapland, the cafes of Paris, the deserts of Israel,
the hashish dens of Afghanistan, the ashrams of India.

The kinds of questions one asks are very powerful, very defining. They will take you in one direction or another. They will create your path in life. Who is your target audience? is one kind of question. It will lead to more questions, to answers, to decisions, to actions, to results.

Who am I? is another kind of question. This kind of question leads only inward to silence and dissolution and to something that cannot be said. That unutterable endlessness is the result of Who am I? It is the true spine of this book, which also happens to be the true spine of us all. That spine, subtle but real, is the channel through which the multicolored primal electricity spews life force to the spiritual centers of our body.

I took Mr. Balsekar's questions to heart. I should not have done so. They were not, and they are not, *my* questions. I should have laughed and fled. Of course, I am grateful to him for tempting me to give up my questions. I don't mind turning left when I should have turned right, if when I realize my error I am more resolved than before to go in the right direction. The vision quest in Mexico restored me to my questions, and them to me. It has been a happy reunion.

Now my answer to Mr. Balsekar is this: a businessman should be interested in truth because first things come first. FIRST THINGS FIRST. You do not ask God to take out your garbage. It is, at least, impolite. You would not put God to work doing your chores and fulfilling your "to do" list, would you? I would guess that if you came home one day to find God sitting in your living room, you would say something

like, "Are you comfortable? Is there anything I can do or get
for you? Another beer, or more salsa?" You would find some
way to serve God. You would find some way to put your own
agenda on hold. The lesser is the servant of the greater.

First things first. Are we businessmen, or are we first
human beings? Are we Democrats or Republicans, or are we
first human beings? Are we Chinese or Tibetan, or are we
first human beings? Are we white or black or red, or are we
first human beings? Are we male or female, or are we first
human beings? Are we Jews or Catholics, Hindus or
Moslems, or are we first human beings? Are we fat or thin,
rich or poor, or are we first human beings?

First things first. We are first human beings. What does it
mean to be a human being? What is the context in which a
human being will be what it is, in truth, in essence, in fact?

Context refers to the circumstances in which an event
occurs and which help determine its meaning, value, and significance.

Jerry Rice, the premier wide receiver in the history of
professional football, plays for the San Francisco 49ers. He
is six feet two inches tall and weighs 200 pounds. Mr. Rice is
of average stature in the context of the National Football
League, where jumbo offensive linemen weigh upwards of
325 pounds. If you were to put Mr. Rice in a jockey's racing
silks and sit him atop a horse, well, suddenly he would be
huge. Don't bet on him to win, place, or show. If you were
to put Mr. Rice in the sumo ring against Grand Champion

Akebono, who weighs 520 pounds, Mr. Rice would be tossed like a salad.

Each context determines the meaning and significance of Mr. Rice's size, according to the purpose, goals, rules, and customs of each context.

Courage on the battlefield means one thing. Battlefield courage may include the readiness to endure tremendous personal deprivation while placing oneself in harm's way without question or hesitation. Courage on a meditation cushion means to remain unmoving against the onslaught of thoughts and feelings as they take their turn pounding your inner brain while your knees and back ache from hours of sitting. This courage is for the sake of seeing where thoughts come from and what they are, and to answer the question "Who am I?"

The meaning and significance of courage, like size, is determined by context.

Now my answer to Mr. Balsekar is that business is not a worthy enough context for living if it, in turn, is not contextualized by life itself, by *being,* by human being. The motto of only-for-profit business is *the business of business is business,* and a business person so engaged is likely to ask "How can I make money?" The first question of a mystic is "Who am I?"; the second question is "How can my business actualize human *being* and serve life?" For the mystic, money is not the goal; money is part of the means by which the far worthier goals of enlightenment and service may be realized. The mystic acts in this way choicelessly; the mystic cannot act outside the context of life and life's commandments.

We need to put ourselves in life's context, so we don't misquote the nature of reality and pervert the truth of who we are and thus wander through life as soulless ghosts. So we must ask the question "What is a human being?" To answer this question will give depth and dimension, value and significance, meaning and purpose to being in business.

———

A few years ago, I accompanied an executive team to the Green Gulch Zen Center in Mill Valley, California for a three-day retreat. Our agenda was to review corporate goals, renew commitments, and strengthen relationships. Well after the first day's session, somewhere around 1:30 a.m., one of the division vice presidents and I began speaking about his recent vacation.

The others had gone to sleep. He and I were sitting on a futon, his face barely visible in the light of the fire's last embers. He told me how one morning he had roused his wife and three sons and how they went together, before the sun was up, to sit on the edge of the rim of the Grand Canyon. They sat together holding hands in silence, their feet dangling in the abyss, watching the sun come up. He tried to say more about that moment but he couldn't.

Instead, his breathing elongated and his eyes narrowed, as though he were seeing into an indescribable distance. I could feel the *presence* within him and surround him. He spread giant wings and yet remained seated and still.

After many silent moments, he said, simply, *I love my family more than anything. I want to live in that love.*

Today I'd tell Mr. Balsekar this is why a businessman would want to read my book. To remember the once known, the twice known, but frequently forgotten essential context of human *being:* I want to live in that love.

Haven't you ever sat with your feet dangling in the cosmic abyss and been consumed by a presence, a force, an encompassing state of being? Here, in the early morning as the sun comes upon the water-crafted canyons, we are able to see without stop, across boundaries into the distance that cannot be spoken. Something is revealed here, some form of wordless knowing that transcends ambiguity and relativity. The word my client used to represent this experience was love. Love is the discovery we make as we engage in spiritual inquiry.

There is no separation within this timeless communion we call love. We know this from our own experience. We all want to live in the love, because it is in this living that we find our wholeness and our totality. In this revelation of our unity with all things, we find a clarity of conscience which will serve as our chief advisor when we are confronted with the dilemmas and challenges of running a business.

As we open to and embrace this power, this presence of love, we forge a new alliance with life and with work. We can depend upon that power to help us make clear and impeccable decisions.

If there is such a thing as the bottom line in spiritual realization, it might be this: You, in your essence, are the bottom line. Nothing else can ever be realized, because nothing else exists.

No one can teach us the answer to this question. Did anyone teach us to breathe? Breathing is a part of us. And so we are; no one can teach us what we are. Still, most of us have forgotten how to breathe the air of our own self, so we must find out who we are.

There is a fantastic absurdity in this. The absurdity is that we usually think we are what we are not. This is what we can learn, this is what can be taught. We can see what we are not, and then we are free to be everything that we are.

Someone can point out that we are not an idea, image, or concept. We are not thought. We are not fear. We are not doubt. We are not confusion. We are not the struggle to figure out what to do or which way to go. We are none of these.

All of what we think we are belongs to the mind. The mind produces our confusion, sadness, loneliness, fear. These, in turn, create the struggles, conflicts, and problems we can never really solve, though our lives are consecrated to their solution.

The solution is to recognize who we are, now, in this moment.

We *Are* What to Do

*A mystic knows without knowledge, without intuition or
information, without contemplation or description or revelation.*
— ATTAR

WE DO NOT HAVE TO FIGURE OUT what to do—we *are* what
to do. We *are* what's next, we *are* the future, now. We are
already whole, clear, powerful. We are love, and in this
knowing we become free. In this freedom we act wisely.

Shortly before my conversation with Mr. Balsekar derailed
my mysticism and business leadership book project, I interviewed Judith Skutch-Whitson, publisher of *A Course in
Miracles*. She told me the following story:

*A long time ago, I was teaching parapsychology at New York
University, and in one of my classes was a young man attached to the
Venezuelan Embassy. We became good friends and one day my young
friend told me that he and the Venezuelan ambassador had some-*

times discussed parapsychology and spirit. He also said that the ambassador wanted to meet me.

At that time, the ambassador was considered to be a mediator par excellence; anytime there was a problem anywhere in the United Nations, he was called upon to mediate the dispute.

One day we met for lunch. He was a silver-haired, dapper gentleman who kissed my hand and made me feel instantly like a queen. We had a grand lunch talking about parapsychology and psychic research. He told me he was very hungry to talk about these things but could not seem to find people in his own environment who had these similar ideas. I told him I knew two people who held a mystic circle in the UN. We each had the feeling that one of the purposes of our meeting was for me to introduce him to like-minded people.

I asked him how he originally got involved in this kind of thinking. He said, "Many years ago, I was sent to France for my education. One of my teachers was an old Jewish philosopher, a very gifted man, who gave me a very precious gift. He taught me how to quiet myself, a method of inner meditation, a process by which I could touch the deep inner core of my being."

I was of course very interested and asked him if he could give me an example of how or when he would do this. He replied, "I had a two-week assignment in Paris. It was a very gloomy winter week and I had to get the leaders of forty-three Third World countries to agree on twenty-four principles of action for the United Nations. There were so many different languages, even many dialects of languages within the contingents of certain countries, and for the first week the meeting was an absolute cacophony of disaster.

"No one was speaking to anyone else. It was dreary and cold. The room wasn't well ventilated and people were smoking and coughing and wheezing and no one was listening to anyone. I felt as if I were a total failure and wondered what to do.

"All of a sudden, the face of the Jewish philosopher appeared before me and I remembered that I had forgotten the precious gift he gave me so many years ago. I had forgotten to do the technique that he had taught me. I closed my eyes for a few moments. I took a few deep breaths and I went deep, deep, deep into my interior where I really live. I asked for help about what to do. A voice said to me Open your eyes and let your eyes go around the room and see each person and surround them with light. I slowly opened my eyes and began to do as I was instructed.

"I looked at each of the delegates, slowly and one at a time, and I surrounded them with light and broadcast the thought I love you.

"It took about half an hour. I was so intent upon my process, that I didn't notice when the level of noise receded. It was very interesting. The delegates began actually talking and listening in a manner that I had not seen during the entire first week. I wondered what I should do next and so I again closed my eyes and took a few deep breaths and asked in the deep interior of my being for guidance. The voice said Ask them all to stop and be silent.

"I opened my eyes and said, 'Ladies and gentlemen, I've been sitting here quietly watching all this go on and I realize that we are not getting anywhere. We have twenty-four issues to decide upon and we haven't yet agreed on even one. I know each of you have cultures which recognize creation as being far greater than the individual person and I know that in your own homes you celebrate that idea. I would like to offer the opportunity of a five minute silence and I would like to ask that everyone touch that part of him- or herself wherein that spirit lives to ask how we might best proceed.'

"No one disagreed. I asked that the lights be dimmed, and we closed our eyes for five minutes. And then the miracle happened. We opened our eyes and that room was filled with light. Everyone saw it and gasped. No lights had gone on, the sun hadn't come out, but that room was full of light.

"Within two hours we had come up with a plan on how to approach the twenty-four issues. We went home two days early, having accomplished our mission."

Here is a man who was much honored for his ability and achievements, and they never knew why. He never told anyone that the source of his skill came from an old Jewish philosopher who had explained to him where our oneness lies, and of how to touch that sacred place.

Twenty-five years ago, I was living in an ashram in India. One morning, around 5:30, I was leaving the kitchen in which I had been cleaning and cutting fruits and vegetables for the communal lunch. The sun was just rising above the mountain ridge across the valley. I sat on a concrete planter that surrounded several coconut trees and fell very silent.

My head became heavy with silence and my body began to disappear, to dissolve. In another moment there was only breathing, not just my breathing—the respiration of the body—but a breathing of everything around me. I entered that breath of all things and disappeared.

In this breath was a white light. It emanated from everything. It was everywhere. The leaves and flowers of plants, stone walls, the clumps of dirt, the muddy water, the people beginning to pass by—awareness of breathing and light, yet no perceiver, no body, no self. And tremendous order and intelligence! Such precision and purpose—each thing related exquisitely to the next—everything defined within itself and in relation to everything else, ordered and sustained by the breathing and the light which had no source but was everywhere, streaming, busy and yet unmoving.

This lasted for two days, after which I did not want to talk for a long time.

The residue of this experience is with me to this day. I know that I embrace all of life within me, and I am embraced by all of life. Sometimes I cry when the utter peace of that light returns. I know the world is a condensation of this breath. We are particles of the light of this breath.

It is this light which gives beauty and significance to all things. It is this light which binds everything together. This light is the breath of love. This light is the consciousness which pervades the entire universe. This is who we are.

Awakening into who we are is the bottom line of spiritual realization. Spiritual realization is not a matter of learning something new. It is not about new insights or experiences or abilities. Realization occurs in a total release of thoughts, images, and reactions. We are not any of these, though they do occur within us. We are that within which these occur. This is what we have to realize.

The constant play in our minds of thoughts, images, and reactions produces hallucinations of identity. We are not these hallucinations.

We are silence and light, and when we know who we are,
we will know what to do.

———————————

There are a few borders to cross on the way to realizing
who we already are. It is ironic to say "on the way to becoming who we already are," but the irony does not have to
compromise the fact that we are who we are, and not who
we think we are.

One of the frontiers is the realization that we do not have
independent, separate lives, though we may think we do. A
separate life is part of our mental hallucination. When we
pass safely through this frontier, our erratic behavior ends.
Our thoughts don't move us. Our fears and urges don't
define us. All of our striving to enhance and perfect the separate self comes to an end.

In a dream, we can see and feel and experience and know
so much. Then we awaken, and smile. Spiritual realization
causes us to smile, too. We are no longer moved by the force
of thoughts or fear or striving to become something.

We are, and have always been, an expression of that
supremely free creative force of pure consciousness from
which everything perceptible and imperceptible is born.
While we experience ourselves in this body and personality
and mind, our real Self extends out the back of us into the
deepest reaches of the universe, speeding through unknow-
able galaxies and dimensions without time.

This is not whimsy. It is a fact. It is real, and being real, it
is the practical and useful antidote for relieving the tension
and confusion and fear of our hallucinated separate existence.

This is what Lao Tzu meant when he said, "Do nothing, and nothing is left undone." I would say it this way: Be who you are and everything is already done.

To be a human being means to drown in silent knowledge and be resurrected in freedom.

Rumi knew such freedom, and he declared, "God has revealed to me that there are no rules for worship. Say whatever your loving tells you to. Through you a whole world is freed. Loosen your tongue. Don't worry what comes out. It's all the light of the spirit."

The shapes of our loving are the truest context for human being. We should become free to speak the truth of silent knowledge in each thing that we do, declaring our real worth, value, and significance.

Why is it so easy for us to forsake this silent beauty? This beauty is the breath that keeps us alive. Our skill should come from this knowing. Our speech should come from this knowing. Our actions should come from this knowing.

We should not fear deep meditation. We should not fear our soul bursting from the constraints of our caution. Who will reproach us for being the light of this clarity? No one, because we are all longing to emerge into this light.

But this knowing is silent. This knowing is a mystery, revealed in the drenching and the drowning. Deep meditation means to suck into our body through the straw of silence the entire ocean of life. We can have no further certainty than this drinking in. One does not need anything but to love this silent knowledge.

Let the silent poetry of this knowledge take our mind, our hands, our tongue. Our secret heart of longing is already taken by this poetry. Turn towards it again and again.

The New Species

No magic bullet, not even the Internet, can save us from population
explosion, deforestation, climate disruption, poison by pollution,
and wholesale extinctions of plant and animal species. We are going
to have to want different things, seek different pleasures, pursue
different goals than those that have been driving us and our global
economy.

— JOANNA MACY

One should not give up, neglect or forget his inner life for a
moment, but he must learn to work in it, with it and out of it,
so that the unity of his soul may break out into his activities.

— MEISTER ECKHART

WE START PLAYING FOLLOW THE LEADER as kids, and we
never stop. Now, as grownups, the game has higher stakes.
Before we give our allegiance to a leader, we need to clearly
understand what we want our leaders to do, and to be. We
can't just blindly follow Susie or Timmy or Johnny or Eliza-
beth because they happen to be at the front of the line. If we
take the time to really investigate the mystique of leader and

leadership, we may find that we ourselves are the leaders we want to follow.

Leadership is like a koan, one of those insoluble Zen riddles that are used to confound the mind and drive one into a spontaneous realization of truth. When you take your hard-won answer to Zen masters, they are likely to bust you over the head in disgust. NOT EVEN CLOSE! Back to the mat you go. Day after day, you bring your answer to the riddle for the Zen master's approval. Day after day, you are rebuked and sent away. No answer or definition will ever be approved. Only a spontaneous outpouring of intuition and freedom will be approved. But we're not Zen students here, so let's attempt some definition of leadership. Maybe we can sneak one by the Zen master.

There are scores of leadership definitions, each with its own set of characteristics, qualities, and goals. Concepts of leadership are constantly evolving as our culture evolves. Any concept of leadership is heavily dependent upon context; leaders are defined and evaluated in terms of their purposes and goals: a military commander wins medals for leadership that would be unthinkable on a mindfulness walk through a meadow. There are over 40 synonyms for leadership in my dictionary, and each one differs significantly in nuances of meaning and context. We could stock a bookstore with books on leadership. We can spend a fortune attending leadership seminars and conferences, listening to audiotapes, and watching video programs that present leading edge techniques, models, theories, and paradigms to develop our leadership potential.

We can try to define leadership with adjectives. Stop by
the business section of your neighborhood bookstore, and
you will find leadership styles of various colors and textures:
visionary, passionate, spiritual, authentic, charismatic, practical.
The pantheon of leadership gurus whose works we can study
include Jesus Christ and Warren Bennis, Machiavelli and
Stephen Covey, Genghis Khan and Margaret Wheatley, Sun
Tzu and Robert K. Greenleaf.

We can try to distinguish leadership from management.
We can say that management is about organizing, planning,
implementing, and controlling; and leadership is about
vision, values, and spirit. Using this distinction, we can go on
and try to refine the characteristics, attitudes, and behaviors
of a leader. Or we might say that a leader can be known only
by their works. A few years ago, an article in the *San Francisco
Chronicle* used a survey of 250 senior executives, showing that
the leadership characteristic held in highest regard was the
ability to get results. Of course, because we so often turn to
leaders to solve our problems.

Even this cursory inquiry into leadership reveals that the
leadership elephant is too big for anyone to get their arms
completely around. Anything we say about leadership can
only be a description of the part of the elephant we are
touching, not the whole elephant.

In our society, a leader is most often defined as having the
kind of authority that either commands or influences people.
The source of that authority might be political or organizational, such as that of a president or governor or CEO. It
might be religious, as in the case of a priest or rabbi. A

leader's authority and influence might come from their wealth or celebrity or social pedigree.

In addition to the obvious leaders, like President Clinton and General Colin Powell, we could say that Bob Dylan and Barbra Streisand are leaders. Bill Gates and Anita Roddick are leaders, as are Susan Sarandon and Martin Scorsese and Jody Foster. Ozzy Osburne and Bonnie Raitt are leaders. Larry Flynt and Jerry Falwell and Louis Farakhan are leaders, as are Michael Jordan and Lisa Leslie and Martina Navratilova. Donna Karan and Giorgio Armani are leaders, as are Oprah Winfrey and Maya Angelou. Deepak Chopra, Bernie Siegel, and Marianne Williamson are leaders. Barbara Walters and Larry King and Howard Stern and Norman Lear are leaders, as is Stephen Hawking.

These leaders—defined by their ability to influence—live in every sector of our society: government, entertainment, business, media, sports, religion, science, education, medicine and health, and the military. These leaders have high visibility, either locally or nationally, and their statements are heard and considered.

The influence that these people have helps to define the reality of those whom they influence. They might define our philosophy and values, our lifestyle, our aesthetic; they might define our product choices, or for whom we vote. They might ask us to open our eyes to new possibilities, or to keep our eyes closed. These leaders, by their words and actions, affect our attitudes about *everything:* politics and foreign policy, money, art, sex, death, race and gender issues, relationships and marriage, ethics and morality, work, diet and health, spirituality, religion, heaven and hell, animal rights, and on and on. In all cases, a leader's influence in some measure defines our reality, whether or not we embrace a particular point of view; rejecting someone's point of view can just as easily help shape and define our values and priorities.

These leaders may be wise and intelligent or they may be ignorant and stupid. They may serve the common welfare, or they may bilk unsuspecting people out of billions of dollars. They may tell the truth, or they may be habitual liars. They may be chaste swans and mate for life, or they may be intrepid sexual adventurers. Having influence is no guarantee of anything; it just means some people will listen and, in many cases, follow.

This last bit is really bothersome. We should expect some guarantees about who and what a leader is. Leaders should be committed to the common good, not just special interests. Leaders should tell the truth. Leaders should consider the short- and long-term consequences of their actions; by short-term, I mean 100 years, and by long-term, I mean 500 years. Leaders should respect life and should serve and protect all living things. Leaders should be creative, able to come up with ideas and solutions that have never been seen or tried before. Where is the great leadership vision and intelligence behind going to war? Haven't we seen the futility of this too many times? Leaders should be curious and continuously learning, they should associate with all kinds of people from many cultures so they can become rich and exotic through diverse influences. Leaders should be comfortable with their bodies; they should be able to enjoy pleasure, and not be the indentured slaves of fear, shame, and guilt. Leaders should explore the spiritual realm of life.

But there is something over and above all of this that we should expect from our leaders.

We should expect them to know reality.

Nisargadatta Maharaj, an Indian mystic, said, "When more people come to know their real nature, their influence, however subtle, will prevail and the world's emotional atmosphere will sweeten up. When among the leaders appear some great in heart and mind and absolutely free from self-seeking, their impact will be enough to make the crudities and crimes of the present age impossible."

We should expect our leaders to know their real nature, and in knowing their real nature, know reality.

Leaders must know their real nature, and the nature of reality. However great may be their leadership skills, abilities, achievements, all is worthless unless they are awake, unless they know their real nature and the nature of reality. This knowledge is the yeast that leavens all other leadership capabilities.

The new species of leader is a hybrid of what used to be two separate species—a mystic and a leader. The new species is a mutant creature, the illicit offspring of a savagely beautiful midnight coupling.

This new species of leader is defined by inner forces of consciousness, not by outer conditions of influence. The new species of leader is a lover of truth and a servant of reality. This new species obsoletes previous species of leader. The difference between the old and the new is one of incalculable orders of magnitude. This new species is ordained by consciousness.

Leaders explore the true nature of self, mind, and reality; their authority derives from this exploration. A leader's mind and heart, a leader's conduct, a leader's spine, are all purified by silence and deep consciousness. A leader is a scout on the frontier of consciousness. A leader's function is to enter the wilderness of reality, to open and clear the way, and to invite and encourage others to likewise explore.

We might want a more concrete definition of the new species, something to wrap our rational minds around, a set of criteria, a list of new species leadership skills, characteristics, and behaviors. But invisible leadership is a koan, and any definition will just create the illusion of knowledge. We have to go beyond the illusion of knowledge to the freedom of being, and in this being discover the truth of leadership. We can't see something we've never seen before with the old eyes and with the old mind. We need new eyes, eyes that see the invisible; we need a new mind, one that can give itself away to that which is greater than itself. We are speaking of a creature whose mother is spirit and whose father is silence, a creature who lives in reality. We cannot understand this, we can only become it in a flash flood of intuitive seeing.

A rabbi, asked to define soul, said: "You know how when you're sleeping and you have a dream which you think is real,

but then you wake up and see that the dream was just a
dream; well, the soul is what we wake up into when we
awaken from being awake." A leader is a person who, while
being awake, wakes up a bit more.

Kabir, a 15th century poet, wrote, "When love hits the
farthest edge of excess, it reaches wisdom. And the fragrance
of that knowledge!" That fragrance is leadership.

The Buddhist monk Thich Nhat Hanh said, "The most
basic precept of all is to be aware of what we do, what we
are, each minute." This awareness is leadership.

The Tibetans have an adage, "Skillful means require
insightful wisdom to produce effective action." Insightful
wisdom is leadership.

The poet Rumi wrote, "A True Human Being is the
essence, the original cause. The world and the universe are
secondary effects." Leadership is the original cause.

The philosopher J. K. Krishnamurti said, "Between two
thoughts there is a period of silence which is not related to
the thought process." Leadership is that silence.

In the Dalai Lama's acceptance speech for the Nobel Peace
Prize a few years ago, he said, "Because we all share this small
planet Earth, we have to learn to live in harmony and peace
with each other and with nature. That is not just a dream, but
a necessity."

This is an important scouting report from the frontier of
consciousness. It is so simple, and yet so critical. *To live in
harmony and peace with each other and with nature* is the first job
of leadership, its top priority and goal.

Wherever we are, we must begin now to live in harmony and peace with each other and with nature. We've got to honestly evaluate our motives and our actions to see if they are in accord with *live in harmony and peace with each other and with nature*. Are we, or are we not, truly and deeply committed to harmony and peace with each other and with nature? If we are not, then we must change. If we are, then let's get on with it. This is a firm line in the sand. It is a nonnegotiable requirement of leadership. There is no middle ground, no political gamesmanship, no public relations spinning double talk that can compromise this.

If we are to establish a new planetary order, we must first establish an equivalent order within ourselves, which can then serve as the foundation for a new order of purpose, values,and ethics in our world. If we are to transform ourselves, and thus the world, we must discover some basic truths about who we are. We must begin to question our ideas and beliefs, not just defend them even as we attack others'. Obviously we must do this, because our old ideas and beliefs have not led us to live in peace and harmony with each other, and certainly not with nature.

We have to travel into the deep interior of our inner consciousness and explore its riches for transformative insights. I think we must go here, into the silence, to find out how we can create a new order. In this silence we will discover the designs needed to realize peace and harmony. In this silence we encounter our unity, in unity we experience peace. This awareness is universal, it is timeless, it is supremely significant.

This state of oneness is a state of true knowledge, of illuminated understanding. When our inner awareness is awakened, we can see that our world of everyday convention is not the real world, but a world of projected thoughts, images, and beliefs. We can see that our problems and sadness and unfulfilled longing for happiness are not facts of life, but are of our own doing. We develop subtle perceptions of cause and effect. We know how and why things are the way they are, and we have the courage and ingenuity to lift up our foundering ship. This *seeing* is leadership.

A bean counter from the parent company had been harassing my client, the president of a manufacturing subsidiary. New product development was behind schedule, and the flagship prototypes were showing serious reliability problems. Costs were mounting and the prospects of quick sales fading. His message was direct and nonnegotiable: time to suck it up and tough it out, time to accomplish more with fewer people in less time. He threatened jobs, salaries, bonuses, stock options, parachutes—anything he could think of to drive the shivering message home. In one meeting, he said, "This is business, dammit, and I want to see blood on the floor and pain on everyone's face."

My client asked me to organize a three-day off-site for his executive team. He wanted me to facilitate their process of figuring out how to lay off 40% of the company. I found a Christian retreat facility in Palo Alto and arranged the details.

During our late afternoon break the second day, I happened to be sitting alone near a huge window that looked out onto the extensive park-like lawn. I was tired and needed a moment of meditation to refresh myself. I began to focus on my breath. My mind, which had been filled with the names of so many people whose fates were being decided, began to follow my breath into the deep inner room of stillness and peace. As my mind becomes still, my senses relax and open to a finer and sharper sensing, my eyes and ears and nose and skin become powerfully intuitive.

I opened the window from the bottom to let in the cool evening air. Breathing slowly, emptying myself, I noticed some birds pecking for worms on the lawn. I saw a spider in its web, waiting, and moist leaves decaying on the ground. I saw insects flitting from here to there. I noticed a very slight subtle rain of pollen, or amber powder, settling on the trees around the perimeter of the grounds and on the grass. There was something out there, in everything. Something was at work where the eyes couldn't quite see, some kind of order, some kind of master plan was working through everything that I could see. *My God,* I thought, *how absolutely perfect and exquisite.*

My attention returned to the room, where the charade of reorganization was going on. Vast sheets of paper were taped to the walls on which we had scribbled numbers and people's names with death crosses marked through them. Parts of the previous days' conversation drifted into my mind, and I burst out laughing, the kind of laughing that is very close to uncontrollable crying. I reviewed the rationalizations for laying off Bill but not Maria, or Linda and not Ted. I listened again to the promises and assurances given to the inquisitors from the head company who dropped by to be sure we were spilling enough blood. These pictures dissolved as I was lured into deeper breathing, deeper meditation.

I again looked outside and felt that a golden presence was spinning wheels just beyond where the eye could see. Everything outside moved together, following a plan that unfolded mysteriously from silence—a natural order that made perfect sense. Outside, in the silence, in the light, an unerring design was being implemented without any harm to the *whole*. Inside, the plans seemed crude and stupid, motivated by greed and fear.

We were almost ready to begin again. The people were returning from the break. They were tired too. A few spoke together, others stood or sat alone, lost in their own thoughts and reveries. I looked outside one last time, and noticed that the light which held everything had gathered at the window and was trying to get in. I don't know how but it did, and it started to fill the room. It seemed that light was trying to get our attention to invite us in.

I intuited that each person in the room *was* linked to that presence which managed the outside world of birds and insects and flowers and spiders, the unhurried world of perfect order and balance and cooperation. I saw that light form a subtle body, a halo, around each of us. If we could notice this light of the perfect plan surrounding us, we would not have to endure the suffering of our lesser plans.

Our new leaders will be able to see these subtle bodies that link us to a more perfect plan than the ones we create with our minds. Leaders will be able to read the wisdom scrolls that unfurl every evening in the amber twilight. Leaders will use that penetrating light to plan and organize and implement their visions with the same prescience that we marvel at in nature's perfection.

It will take some time for us to install such leaders within the hierarchies of our corporations and institutions. In the meantime, I suggest that every such organization hire a mystic to serve as Vice President of Consciousness to help in the transition. These positions could be filled with such people as Huston Smith, Ram Dass, Thich Nhat Hanh, Marianne Williamson, Joanna Macy, Barbara Marx Hubbard, Caroline Myss, John Robbins, Stephen Levine, Shakti Gawain, Riane Eisler, Jerry Jampolsky, Brother David Steindl-Rast, Jean Shinoda Bolen, Jean Houston, Matthew Fox, Joseph Goldstein, Rabbi Harold Kushner, Jack Korn-field, Louise Hay, and Joan Borysenko. From their works these candidates seem sufficiently expert in matters of consciousness and conscience, courage and compassion, intel-ligence and wisdom to be the trustees of the transition from the old species of leader to the new. There are many, many more such qualified candidates, though they may not yet be considered in terms of corporate and organizational leader-ship. Find them, hire them, learn from them. Let them tutor and inspire us. Let their current of deep living infiltrate every corner of our organizations. We shouldn't let our pride, arro-gance, or vanity get in the way.

The mystic's mandate, as a senior executive on the transi-tion team—in addition to teaching the ways and means of mystical realization—is to challenge motives, question research, require accountability, insist upon the highest good.

The other executives must listen and respond to them
without turning away or stonewalling. These VPs would not
be bound by corporate agreements of secrecy or oaths of
loyalty. They would be free at any time to reveal the inner
workings of the decision-making machinery. These VPs are
monuments to awareness and truth, reminders of the invisible world in which we live and work.

After years of meditation and contemplation of the true
nature of self, mind, and reality, mystics will not get lost
in the mind's hall-of-mirrors, but remain anchored to the
shock-absorbing rebar that girds the Earth's core. They will
not be seduced by the perks of power nor swayed from a
clear seeing of actions and consequences. They are to affirm
the sacredness of life and assure that all activities are in com-
pliance with such a sacred view. What does sacred mean? It
refers to the mystical fact that everything is conscious, everything feels, thinks, suffers. Everything is dependent upon
everything else for its well-being, and everything is entitled
to live and prosper in happiness and safety. The sacred view
is to care for everything in the extreme. The sacred view
does not exploit anything for profit, comfort, or conve-
nience. When these mystic executives sense pollution or
degradation, another way must be found. Their mandate
is to safeguard the ecosystem of living beings, to promote
awareness, to inspire compassionate action.

Please, let us do this, let us embrace and enfold those
among us who have dedicated their lives to awareness and
consciousness. Let us admit that our secular leadership has
failed. Let us admit that we must quickly establish a regime
of sacredness. As in all times of crisis, change, and transition,

there will be protests and denials, difficulties and sorrow, sacrifice and loss. Let us trust captains of mysticism to help us
navigate this turbulent time; they can show us how to turn
our earth-ship to the port or starboard and avoid the Titanic's
fate.

Let us listen to the mystics who speak for the wisdom of
our hearts, that we may find within us what we know, what
we cherish, what we love, but often forget. Let our leaders
be those among us who remember, and let us all remember
so we may all become leaders.

White House Voodoo

Disbelief in magic can force a poor soul into believing in government and business.

— TOM ROBBINS

The lion's swift attack is the right punishment for those who insult the spirit, for those who find a pure stream and then urinate in it.

— RUMI

THERE WAS QUITE A BROUHAHA after Bob Woodward revealed in his book *The Choice* that Jean Houston had facilitated some visualizations for Hillary Clinton.

Mr. Woodward mentions in his book that the Clintons had invited a group of communications and popular self-help authors, including Anthony Robbins, Marianne Williamson, and Stephen R. Covey, to Camp David. But it is Jean Houston—described as "an attractive woman with long, dark hair and a large, generous smile" wearing "an ancient Hellenistic coin of Athena set in a medallion around her neck all the time"—and her colleague Mary Catherine Bateson who receive most of Mr. Woodward's attention. Even so, the references are fairly brief.

Possibly these passages or Mr. Woodward's subsequent appearances on various television interview shows lit the fire. Over the course of several weeks, the firestorm of controversy generated numerous stories and media appearances by several of the protagonists of this drama. But the thing which needed to be said was never said.

Mr. Woodward spoke about his book with Stone Phillips on NBC's *Dateline*. The conversation turned to the matter of Jean Houston and her work with Mrs. Clinton, and Mr. Phillips had the look of someone who had either just seen a ghost or glimpsed the Second Coming. He acted incredulous at what he was hearing. *They did WHAT?* Mr. Woodward also seemed to enjoy the preposterousness of what had occurred.

In my own way, I was as incredulous as Mr. Phillips seemed to be, but not at Jean Houston and Hillary Clinton. I was incredulous at Mr. Phillips and Mr. Woodward, from whose reactions one would have thought that the First Lady had cavorted nude and mud-soaked under a full moon, instead of delighting in the very modest and rudimentary visualization techniques she actually practiced.

Their reactions reminded me of how reactionary our culture is in terms of consciousness and reality. I mulled over a new term: *consciousness fascism.*

According to my dictionary, fascism is a system of government marked by centralization of authority under a dictator and suppression of the opposition through terror and censorship. Consciousness implies awareness of reality. Guided by these definitions, consciousness fascism might be the terroristic suppression and censorship of awareness, of reality, by the dictator of ignorance. Consciousness fascism is endemic and epidemic in precisely those sectors of society most in need of expanded consciousness: government, media, and business.

Spiritual development is not an option. The enhancement of one's awareness through mystical experience is unequivocally prerequisite for leadership, just as it is for any intelligent, creative, effective, and truthful living. We must not follow, listen to, be influenced by, or in any way empower or legitimize any person who is not forging strong links to reality through meditation, self-inquiry, or other contemplative practices. Mystics must not be marginalized in society or defamed by those whose power is rooted in egoistic delusions and who, in the name of those delusions, serve only the specialized interests of power, greed, and fear through repressive and corrupt policies and practices.

We are so hypnotized by the pettiness and frivolity of our consumer- and entertainment-based culture, so corrupted by the influence of money, power, and technology, so obsessed with celebrity and self-interest, so persuaded by politics and science, so victimized by sheer inattention and foolishness that many of us don't learn what must be learned until it is either almost too late, or too late. That is why we learn most in times of crisis, why we seem to awaken only in the presence of some catastrophic sadness. It is then that we are jolted out of our trance to see how puny and inconsequential our self-centered ideas and beliefs and pursuits are.

We do not have time to tolerate the leadership of ignorance any longer. We must not allow any more Don Quixotes to decide our fate and the fate of our world, already teetering on the brink of preventable suicide. We do not have time to indulge the same quality of consciousness that consumes, develops, and butchers everything for its own enjoyment. We must uplift, refine, and irradiate our consciousness with mystical understanding—right now, right this minute. If you are already doing this, if you are a true leader, a secret mystic, a closet ecstatic, a friend of reality, and a lover of truth, then you must come forward now. Please do not hide any longer. Please do not equivocate the truth of mysticism.

Last year, a magazine publisher asked me to write an article responding to his question: "What should a good leader think about?" I began that article by saying that leaders already think too much; they should stop thinking and seek truth. I said that leaders should give themselves totally, fully, and completely to the search for truth, without apology or embarrassment; they should become mystics—people who experience truth intuitively. All other leadership attributes, however important they may be, are secondary.

Now, in the aftermath of the birth of the new species of leader, I would assume that all leaders are mystics, already fully committed to truth, reality, and consciousness. I would assume they know how to rely on awareness and intuition. I would assume they already know how to use thought judiciously, as a tool, and not abuse it nor be abused by it. But let's remember the importance of seeking truth.

Seek truth all the time. Seriously, deeply, profoundly, and without surcease. Seeking truth must become a second breath for us: we must breathe truth-seeking through the lungs that connect us to others, to the world, to the worlds beyond this world, to the invisible playgrounds of cosmic forces. These truth-seeking lungs are behemoth organs that oxygenate us with wisdom: our minds with clarity, our actions with integrity, our feelings with compassion. Seek truth.

When it is time to plan, do so. When it is time to decide, do so. When it is time to commit, do so. When it is time to act, do so. But do not ever stop seeking truth. Do you stop breathing when you plan, decide, commit, and act? No! Neither should you stop seeking truth. Seek truth and never stop.

I was recently advisor to a group of people who were growing their consulting and training company into an institute of broader scope and service capability. My role was to stimulate their thinking and contemplation of issues toward greater clarity, toward deeper truth. We were scrutinizing a sentence in their values statement, trying to determine its underlying import and veracity. Finally, one participant blurted out, "It's time to put this to bed. This is just splitting hairs. The average person in the street will not notice these subtleties."

I responded, "But we are not asking these questions for the benefit of the average person on the street. We are asking them so we will know for ourselves what we are actually and truthfully intending to create. We are making the effort to become clear."

Still unconvinced, he replied, "Fine, but there is a time when you stop seeking truth and just get on with it."

I said, "Seeking the truth *is* getting on with it."

This person's response is not unusual: we can become impatient with continual questioning, irritable with prolonged examination of assumptions, angry at clarifying intentions and meanings. Though he knows in theory the value and importance of seeking the truth, he was reluctant to dive into it fully, to fully explore his own intentions. He must know out of what fabric his motivations are woven, he must know what he is doing.

It is difficult to train ourselves to pay attention to the subtle underpinnings of our actions, those potentially obscuring attitudes and assumptions which disrupt our union with the mystic. But we must pay attention to the quality of mind that is about to launch rocks into still ponds. We must know if there are lurking fears or secret ambitions that cloud our discrimination.

So, we must become patient, balanced, and calm, because a leader is a truth-seeker who never stops cultivating awareness, clarity, and truth.

What does seeking truth mean? It means to question everything with skillful, artistic persistence. It means that we always push against our certainty—of assumptions, knowledge, commitments, values, identities, philosophies. To question is to seek truth, and leaders must ask questions that pertain to realms bigger than business. They must seek truth in territory larger than that defined by organization, product, market, pricing, manufacturing, and advertising. Truth-seeking questions are profoundly beautiful and soul-stunning in their implications.

Here are some truth-seeking questions: *Who am I? What am I doing? Why am I doing it? How am I doing it? Who will benefit? Who will be harmed? What might be the consequences of my actions upon generations yet to come? What are beliefs and what do I believe? How are beliefs different from reality? What is real? What is power? What is death? From where does the fire in the belly of my ambitions come? Why do I react the way I do? Can one really achieve security? What is success? What is money and its right use? What does freedom mean? What is love?*

In questioning, go deep. Develop stamina. Practice. Become resilient, strong, unwavering and implacable. Become a genius of questioning. In seeking truth, explore everything. Touch every grain of sand on a billion beaches of exploration and inquiry.

Seeking truth is potent, and it keeps us flexible, fluid, and free, lithe figures dancing in beautiful constellations of incomparable symmetry, permeable by life's infinite mystery and beauty. A leader is one who wears the crown of life's mystery and beauty.

Leaders love epiphanies, sudden monsoons of intuitive perception, revelatory manifestations of consciousness. Epiphanies disturb our cherished assumptions and beliefs about life, and disrupt our conditioned, mechanical patterns of behavior.

Epiphanies come to us through a variety of means: by intentional practice, an accident, a sudden reversal of fortune, the death of a loved one, a confrontation with our own mortality, or by divine grace. Another way in which epiphanies may appear in our lives is through an encounter with a mystic, a living conduit of pure consciousness.

I experienced an epiphany of this last kind a few years ago at the Mt. Madonna Center in Watsonville, California. It is

a retreat facility founded by Baba Hari Dass, an Indian yogi
who has not spoken a word since 1952. I was facilitating a
planning session for a management team of a computer chip
manufacturing company. I had arranged a private meeting
with our group and Baba Hari Dass, who communicates
succinctly and humorously by writing on a chalkboard. We
visited with him for about 30 minutes, asking a variety of
questions, including several about spirituality in business.
When our time was over, I went to thank him. A force
emanated from his eyes that I had experienced in the eyes
of my teacher many years earlier. It was a ray that could
penetrate very deeply into the core of one's being: it is the
touch of reality, or grace, and one awakens to another world
of significance.

As I walked outside with our group I suddenly felt very
strange, light-headed, and off balance. I told my associate to
continue without me, that I would catch up. I wandered into
a grove of trees, found a boulder, and sat down. Something
pierced my heart. I bent over and started crying. It's very
hard to say what occurred to me then. It is probably difficult
for all of us to speak of these moments—so full of silence
and beauty and awakening.

When I stopped crying, I sat still for a long time.
Everything about me seemed newly alive, radiant, as though
I was seeing these common things for the first time: flowers,
trees, rocks, dirt. It seemed that everything was breathing!
I felt light and spacious, extending beyond the familiar
boundary of my body. I became aware of an orderly connection between things, much as when you finally piece a puzzle
together you see how each piece fits into the other to form

the whole. I was relieved of a burden I didn't know I was carrying. I was embraced by a profound peace.

When these disruptions to our conventional way of living occur, it's as though we see another dimension of life about which we were ignorant. The mask of appearances falls away, and we see something profound about life. We experience something of the timeless, the real, that which gives radiance to us in the womb. It's beyond words, and the mind hardly grasps it. In these moments, the fortifications against the soul dissolve, and a new perspective appears.

When we are quiet and open, we can hear the conversations of animals and birds, even plants, stones, and soil. Everything is alive, everything feels joy, and everything feels pain. When we are touched by grace, we become naturally empathetic and kind. Epiphanies remind us that it is not right to turn a blind eye to or profit from someone's suffering or misfortune. We shouldn't forget this just because we might make a lot of money by doing so.

Leaders should gorge on silence. Leaders should love inspiring collisions with the spirit; they should welcome mystical perceptions with wild abandon. Leaders should learn how to play the furious and wordless jazz of that silence which blows life into all things.

One does not come to insight and wisdom through reason, which can only persuade or convince, not intoxicate. Our reasoning cannot reach silence nor touch the soul, it can only grease the gears and pulleys of the mind.

The soul needs another lubricant; the soul needs to feed—
no, to feast—on inspiration. Gorging on inspiration, the soul
explodes in love. To know what must be known about ourselves, we must catapult from all that is reasonable. Leaders
will know that inspiration *is* practical, Self knowledge *is* relevant, love *is* essential.

Let us be taken by silence into the vital part of ourselves,
perhaps forgotten, perhaps ignored, but compelling beyond
reason. The living wholeness of our Self is found in silence,
and silence should be the language of leaders.

Let this silence and this love of the Self affect us, take us,
overwhelm us. Let us give ourselves to this as to music, to
reverie, to beauty. Let the silence that we are create a cata-
clysm of clarity in our lives.

Let our doubts and confusion meet this living wholeness.
Let our rage and torment meet this living wholeness. Let our
unquenchable cravings meet this living wholeness. Let our
efforts to bring peace into our lives and into the world meet
this living wholeness, the sacred Self of all whose name is
love, creator of the universe.

The supreme silence, the primordial essence, the breathing spirit is crawling at warp speed through every tree's
sap-channel and through every lovely child's mystery; it
shapes the calls of wild dogs, and blesses the collapse of stars
as they sip their own mortality. Let us celebrate and remember that we *are* that silence.

Weird Failures

*We sense that there is some sort of spirit that loves birds and the
animals and the ants—perhaps the same one who gave a radiance
to you in your mother's womb. Is it logical you would be walking
around entirely orphaned now? The truth is, you turned away
yourself, and decided to go into the dark alone. You've forgotten
what you once knew; that's why everything you do has some weird
failure in it.*

    — K A B I R

*This is about Richard Nixon. People are dying because he didn't
make the varsity football team. The Constitution is hanging by
a thread because he went to Whittier, and not to Yale.*

    — J. T. W A L S H, as John Ehrlichman in *Nixon*

THE DOORS TO THE INVISIBLE WORLD of our soul are closed
early, when we are inoculated against its wildness. From the
time the doors close, we live on in a deathly darkness, like
those poor souls in Plato's cave who were chained to the
ground facing the cave-walls. They could see only the dim
and smokey figures created by the fire, and believed them to

be the sum total of reality. Every so often, a daring person or two would manage to break free and find freedom, where the real world would crash upon them like a tidal wave of joy. They'd return to the others, but none would believe the stunning reports. People become leaders when they break free from the chains of ignorance and dive into the tidal waves of joy, when they smash open the darkening doors that have been shuttered and locked, inhibiting the soul from bursting out.

One day at an airport, I was reminded of how the doors close upon the daring freedom of the soul's passions and exuberance, of how we get into trouble for dreaming aloud the songs of the invisible world. In the lounge, waiting for the boarding call, was a young girl of about three, maybe four years old. She had a glorious bright look. Energy and enthusiasm would rise within her like waves, and then pound the shore of a chair or corridor or window in excited fits of restlessness. Her life welled up from deep within her, unconditioned and unafraid, raw and vital. It was beautiful. Waves of great soul force shook her with tenderness. She must have dreamed beautiful dreams. I am sure she knew the blessings of her mystical ancestors and played with subtle beings from other dimensions, just as many of us did before we were reprimanded by the call of the fierce world. Her doors were wide open, stressing the hinges.

A door closed. "Jennifer, come here!" said her mother. She wasn't angry, just distracted, but her tone was sharp, and became sharper, with a hint of punishment. She seemed like a good person who was simply distressed by her daughter's tidal waves of joy.

Another door closed. "Don't do that!"
Then another. "Be careful."
Another. "Be quiet."
"Stand still."
"Don't bother people."

Within five minutes, so many doors closed that I wondered how the poor girl would ever open them all again: *stay
here, be good, don't fidget, be quiet, be careful, come back here, don't
do that, don't touch that, stand still, listen to what I tell you, don't
make me angry.* This is no insignificant anecdote. It has happened to all of us. The mother's commands hit the little girl
with forbidding force, a punch of fear and dread. Her little
body froze with each command, shocked and traumatized.
With each trauma, her subconscious mind seemed to whirr
and decide: I will never do *this* again. The little girl did not
need to be physically hit to be hurt, to be cut by the authoritative commands. Within the subterranean processes of her
thoughts and feelings she decided it was not a good idea to
anger her meal ticket of security, love, and approval.

This is what happens. Once *we* turn from the spirit, there
is no end to the turning away that we then demand and
expect from others. With each humiliation, with each embarrassment, with each shocking abuse, we *decide,* and those
decisions become festering wounds. With each decision, we
shape and mold ourselves into a form, an ego, a pattern of
identity and response based on a suppression of our inner life
and its impulses. We turn from radiance to darkness, from
joy to sorrow, from depth to shallowness—each turn creating
momentum, until we become permanently disfigured: dizzy
and confused, fearful and ashamed, obedient and numb.

These closing doors separate us from our natural exuberance, our unique expression of the creative life force: we turn against our own enthusiasm, wonder, awe, curiosity, playfulness, and connectedness to others. As the doors close, we become diminished in spiritual clarity and capacity. We suppress and deny those tidal waves of spontaneous energy and enthusiasm and joy because we learn they may jeopardize our safety and security. Many of us have not yet unlearned that lesson, but we must. This is the inner work that leaders must do to regain the trust and friendship of reality.

With the first blow, the first bruise, we begin to take our instructions from outside, from others. We start taking notes on how it is, what is permissible, what is appropriate. We fill mental note pads with the authoritative teachings of those who have come before us, who themselves learned and now teach that only the dirty, smokey figures on the cave-wall are real. We become inoculated against our own inner force, and day by day we lose our luster and light. Like cheetahs and gazelles, we are stolen away from the natural velds of our true home and put in crates and cement-block cells and display cases. Our self-betrayal begins here, when we believe without question what we are told, when we begin to obey and turn from our own radiance. It can begin even on our very first day in the world.

One of my clients experienced regular emotional upsets, which translated into frequent breakdowns of his work commitments. He asked me to work with him, to help him find out why he lived in such a way.

It didn't take long, because he was ready to change. He broke free during a period of meditation and deep breathing which returned him to the moment of his birth. He remembered his mother's disappointment that her child was a boy, and she said to the doctor *I don't want to hold him. I wanted a girl. Take him away.*

His mother was not greatly interested in him, and he had to learn techniques and tactics to attract her attention and love. He did that by creating upsets and breakdowns in his young life. The attention he got, though it was often negative and harsh, was better than nothing. He thought this attention was love. He magnetized negative attention, confusing that with love.

My client began to separate himself from his mother's comment; he no longer used it as the basis of his self-image. He was able to glimpse who he was before all this distortion and awkwardness; he began to see his original face, as the grit and grime was cleaned from his eyes.

I worked with a very successful businessman who thought he was soul-less. He had refused a missionary assignment from his church and had subsequently been excommunicated. He was told that the church would repossess his soul, and he would live out his life soul-less and bereft of God's love and grace. Maybe it was the church, not my client, which was soul-less and bereft of God's love. But my client believed the church, and lived accordingly.

I can't remember seeing anyone so uptight, nervous, and edgy. On the one hand, he behaved like an existentialist mob boss, pushing his way to the front of every line to grab more than his share, stepping hard on everyone. Why not? If I can't get into God's heaven and experience eternal heavenly

delights, then I'm for goddamn sure going to get everything
I can here and now.

On the other hand, something in him did not believe his
church. He told me *I've got everything. But it's killing me. Living
this way...it's killing me. Even if God has forsaken me, I haven't
forsaken God.*

With that realization, he broke free and was swept out by
a tidal wave of joy. Later, we designed a ritual so that he could
repossess his soul from his church. He, too, found his original
face in the mirror of his own heart, opened again as on the
first day of creation.

A bank executive revealed a pattern he was aware of but
couldn't break. His life would slowly escalate in an easy,
beautiful, fulfilling manner, and then suddenly he would step
on a land mine of adversity, throwing everything out of
balance, challenging him to become heroic. The land mine
might be within himself, an emotional upheaval or physical
sickness. The crisis might be in his family, in the bank, with
his employees, or with some project or investment he was
responsible for. He would have to gather himself up, rouse
his strength and intelligence, and hurl himself at the crisis.

He wanted to see why he couldn't stay longer in the ease,
openness and grace that he knew. He was almost six and a
half feet tall, and seemed to others infinitely strong and confi-
dent. He had been like that as a child. Throughout his life,
his sheer size and charisma inspired people to turn to him in
times of crisis. He received great approval for the times when
he solved problems, overcame adversity, ended a crisis or
conflict. He earned his validation as a person by overcoming
adversity for himself and for others. When there was nothing

to solve or fix, he had no means to experience his power, potency, and worthiness. He could not live for long in peace, because he did not know how to experience himself fully, at peace. So, whenever the balance became too acute, something in his psyche would toss magic dust into the world to create a problem. He could then fix it, and feel alive.

All of my consulting work is about these weird failures. That is not, of course, my clients' initial request, which is usually about some collapse of leadership or breakdown of personal or team communication and performance. In truth, their problems are always about their weird failures projected into the world without their conscious knowledge.

The external world is the reflection of our inner discord, a picture of our hurt, and pain, and fear, and anger. Leaders know this and dedicate themselves to restoring themselves to their spiritual essence, so that the spiritual essence can become realized in the reflective neutrality of the world-canvas.

I was meeting with a client who was a corporate president, to prepare for a senior management team retreat on organizational effectiveness. We had just reviewed my summary of interviews with his executive team, and the feedback about his leadership had brought our conversation to a pause. Some of what people had to say was flecked with anger, disappointment, and frustration. I had presented it as it was told to me, and I also tried to transmit the emotional energy of the senior team members. He was shaken.

After some silence, we resumed our conversation, and my client turned from business matters to extremely personal ones. He explosively defended himself against what he perceived to be a personal attack, in the face of which he felt betrayed and unappreciated.

He leaned forward in his chair, shaking with emotion. *When they need help, don't I take care of them? Don't I help them? When they make mistakes, don't I forgive them? But who forgives me? Who helps me? Who will take care of me?*

I remained silent while he wept. I had seen him approach this threshold before, but not cross it. Now that he had, the real issues were clear, and they had nothing to do with the company or his leadership. The issues were sadness, despair, loneliness, and fear. These are often the real concerns everywhere, and the problems we want to fix are just symptoms of these more elemental issues. Perhaps he was really asking what many of us ask and spend our lives trying to answer: Who will love me?

There are weird failures all around us, and we all suffer because of them. We externalize these failures and then try to solve the problems. The problems remain. No one really knows what to do. The more we try to solve the problems, the more the weird failures seem to proliferate. The weird failures are symptoms of turning from our radiant soul into a world of forgetfulness, of shadowy threats and taunts, of intimidations. These exist, however, only in our minds as stab and burn wounds, terrible scars of being ripped like babies from our resting place of spiritual truth. It is as though we have a Grand High Inquisitor seated on a dais in our brain forbidding us to speak of the invisible world where the radiant being of our true essence shines. As Kabir said, the one who gave us our radiance in the womb has not abandoned us, we have abandoned it. And it *is* us, in our essence.

This is what Kabir was talking about. There is something we have all forgotten, and that forgetfulness makes us heavy and sad. It makes us anxious and fearful and angry. The weird failures have to do with forgetting who we are, with turning away from the spirit which gives us radiance. This alienation causes us to suffer, and we act out that suffering in the world. The world's chaotic and brutal throes are our screams of alienation and forgetfulness. The chaos in the world persists because we have not yet faced ourselves with the sincere intent to heal and become whole again.

"Each of us must be the change we want to see in the world," said Gandhi. In order to be the change we want to see in the world, we must look deeply inward and know ourselves as we are, in our essence. This essence will put an end to the chaos.

Perhaps nations go to war for no other reason than that some president or general was unloved as a child. Holocausts happen every day in the name of commerce or national security or scientific research. We unwittingly inflict the same damage on others, and the world, that we have had inflicted on us. The recent Gulf War is but one example of this. During this conflict, our leaders of that time prepared us for the war by telling us that we were going to go over to Iraq and "kick some ass."

The invasion of Iraq was preconditioned a long time ago by leaders whose pain and anger crept from their hiding places to burrow just beneath the earth's crust as land mines of mischief.

A decade before the current showdown over weapons of mass destruction, the United States turned a blind eye when Iraq used American intelligence for operations against Iran that made rampant use of chemical weapons and ballistic missiles, according to senior Clinton administration and former intelligence officials. The attacks against civilian and military targets during the Iran-Iraq War included some of the most pervasive uses of chemical weapons anywhere since World War I. (The Los Angeles Times, 2/16/98)

So too was the invasion of Panama.

When George Bush became director of the CIA in 1976 under President Ford, he inherited Noriega as a contact. Despite evidence that Noriega was involved in drug trafficking, Bush kept Noriega on the payroll. In fact, he increased Noriega's salary to more than $100,000.00 a year and eliminated a requirement that intelligence reports on Panama include information on drug trafficking. (The Panama Deception)

People whose weird failures are not healed inevitably re-create their pain as tragic world events. They will create the preconditions for these tragedies, because they cannot create the preconditions for peace, justice, and harmony. They do not know these for themselves. Wherever there is abuse of power, fraud, corruption, violence, lying, deception, and repression of freedom, know that there is soullessness. The history of war is the history of soullessness.

This is why we need leaders who will return to their
original radiance.

Leaders have to reclaim their souls, and to do so they will
have to enter themselves deeply to heal and forgive. In order
to reclaim the radiance from which they have turned, they
must understand how their beauty is pummeled and how
they become alienated from their souls. They must understand how soul alienation corrupts their minds with fear and
anger, and how those emotions become their calling cards.
They cannot live in their reasons and justifications: those are
only masks. If they remain the puppets of buried decisions,
how can they ever create new behavior, new solutions?

Only leaders who heal their pain and anger and alienation
will be able to precondition the world for inspiring, life-
affirming, unifying world events.

A client of mine told me the real reason he goes fly-fishing
in the Sierras. He didn't particularly care for fishing, but he
said it was an acceptable excuse to stand all day thigh-deep
in the comforting current of a mountain stream, surrounded
by trees and rocks and clouds. Stillness and silence. Finding
peace while learning the dialects of nature.

He loses himself while standing in the streams of the
Sierras. The beauty and silence of nature draw out his soul
and liberate him from the anxiety and pressures of life.

He says that the top of his head opens and something of him flies up and out and finally hooks in the mouth of a fish swimming in eternity.

And yet he could not directly face this, could not directly admit his yearning for this communion. He pretended to love fly-fishing. He didn't just admit that he hiked into the mountains to feel his soul and connection to fish swimming in eternity.

Many of us are secretive about our longing to unite with the larger beauty of which we are a part. Why are we embarrassed to admit that we want to live in this pristine wilderness of spiritual communion?

What impact might this man have if he could return to his work as the president of a high-tech company trailing the billowing clouds of his soul on a string wrapped around a finger so as not to forget. Sitting at his desk in his office, wouldn't he be as open as the mountain skies, as honest as the trees, as articulate as the stream, as patient as a seedling awaiting the right time?

To touch him anywhere would be to feel the pulse of that gorgeous and picturesque consciousness that imbues the streams in the Sierras with unending delight.

Until we understand our weird failures, we are nothing but terrorists to ourselves and others, brutalizing the world to compensate for soullessness. Without the deep feeling and awareness of what life is, of what we are in our original nature, there can be no love, no joy, no peace in this world. We will seek compensation from the world for the dents to our soul, the blows to our heart. We can never be sufficiently compensated. We cannot make the world pay for our spiritual loss; we must recover for ourselves what was "lost." We must look to where our lost soul still lives, waiting to be found again. We must find each dent, each bruise, each decision, and heal each one with the light touch of love, compassion, and understanding.

Shooting Galleries

Attachment is the great fabricator of illusions; reality can be attained only by someone who is detached.

— S I M O N E   W E I L

When the ego is abandoned, there is only silent awareness, total presence. This silent presence frees us from the patterns fabricated by the ego, thus opening out before us a whole new world of energies.

— J E A N   K L E I N

I T   I S   E A S Y   T O   S E E   T H E   P O C K M A R K E D, desperate face of addiction in crack houses and heroin shooting galleries in the devastated Dresdens of America's inner cities. It is not so easy to see the same depleted face in the mirror of addictions to ideas, power, wealth, celebrity, work, religion, anger, self-pity, possessions. But these are every bit as mean and corrosive to our spirit and to our soul as are crack and heroin and hopelessness.

An addiction refers to anything we do or use habitually to provide a sense of well-being. Often we are not even aware that we have an addiction. We think we are always in control, that we can do or not do, use or not use as we choose. This is not the case. Very few of us are free from addictions. In fact, most of us are defined by addictions we don't even know we have. We can't give them up because we have become our addictions. We hardly know who we are without them.

Leaders will have to face their addictions and overcome them. They will have to pass through the trials of withdrawal in order to become free. Freedom and reality are mirror and image, image and mirror. Where there is reality, there is freedom; where there is freedom, there is reality—this is all that is necessary for well-being.

Charles Grodin said that the media will do anything for a good story. Heroin addicts will do anything for a good fix. They are incapable of being responsible and evaluating the consequences of their actions—to themselves and others— they cannot see how their own illness enters and contaminates the pond of our common existence. Heroin addicts are not free; they cannot choose, cannot do the right thing, cannot see anything in perspective, cannot be generous and kind. Heroin addicts act compulsively. They cannot sit quietly in deep meditation until the true action comes about from silence, from reality. Heroin addicts cannot be trusted; we know they will do anything for their next fix. They are not creative, compassionate, intelligent, intuitive, just, truthful, or accountable. They cannot contribute meaning, beauty, and significance to themselves, others, society, or the world. This is why we hate them. But we ought not hate them until we have looked into our own mirrors. Many of us may be just like the heroin addicts we hate, although our addictions may be socially sanctioned, and therefore invisible.

Are people in the media addicted to a "good story"? Can they turn from a story if their conscience, if their soul, tells them to? This is a serious issue for leaders. Leaders must be free, addicted to nothing, serenely detached, able to walk away or stay forever. Leaders must be free to be used by reality, not by their addictions. Leaders will not depend upon anything other than reality for their well-being, for their identity, for their purpose, for their welfare. Leaders will never be compromised by money, celebrity, fame, power, vengeance, pride, arrogance, vanity, anger, jealousy. Leaders, unlike addicts, are never compulsive, hurtful, deceitful, and destructive. Leaders will not rely on artificial means for their highs in life. Leaders must be willing to recover their freedom from any addictions, from any cravings of insufficiency, which they may have.

A leader's belly is full, a leader's heart is at peace, a leader's mind is content—all from loving reality.

———————

We may think of dependency in terms of substances or relationships. But let's look deeper. What happens when we can't watch our favorite television program? When the morning paper isn't delivered, or the hot water heater breaks? How agitated do we become during a power failure, when the lights and computers and phones stop working?

Do we view our normal expectations as addictions? If the test of addiction is the trauma of deprivation, can we face the enormity of our addictions? What about our very life? When we contemplate our death, do we do so serenely, with understanding and openness? If one is sincerely trying to live freely, creatively, we must wonder about all of this, and try to find out if we can live without the trauma of deprivation stalking us from the shadow of our craving.

We are propped up in a hundred ways that we don't notice. We are addicted to our view of reality. We are addicted to our religious beliefs, without which we would be lost. Our identities and roles and beliefs are all addictions, aren't they? Can we give everything up and be free? Are we not addicted to having our own way, to imposing our will on events? Are we not addicted to our past?

If we look at addiction in this larger view, who is not an addict? Is a politician not addicted to power? Is an evangelist not addicted to rhetoric? Is a scientist not addicted to proof? Is a business person not addicted to profit?

It is a shock to see our own addictions. If everything we depend on were taken away, who would we be? Are we not addicted to our own self-centeredness? Are we not dependent on the events of our lives to give us a sense of coherence and meaning? Are we not addicted to thinking, to projecting our fears and anxieties into the future? Don't we look to our accomplishments for a sense of pride? Can we live without this? Let's be honest, and look precisely at the whole issue of addiction, how we depend on something to keep us intact.

An addict will do anything for the next fix. Will we? How much hostility, violence, and greed do we rationalize in the name of our unexamined addictions? An addict will do any-

thing. Isn't so much of our compulsive, chaotic existence
manufactured by our addictions?

Sitting silently, can we see the first impulse of craving? It
takes courage and honesty to see our whole predicament;
otherwise, we will remain enslaved. We fight so hard for
freedom from external oppression, should we not want to
be equally free from internal oppression, from the slavery
of compulsion and craving?

If we can see and know that moment when craving is
absent, we will understand addiction and what to do about
it. Have you ever sat in a forest at night, unafraid, bathed in
moonlight, listening to the Earth's breathing and the leaves
dancing on the hard earth? Something opens within us, and
this opening is empty and solid at the same time. Profound
stillness of mind. A quivering in the heart of what is wordlessly present. In this depth of being, without movement,
utterly still, is a total absence of craving and dependence.
Returning to silence, to our source, reveals our wholeness,
and in wholeness we become free.

Have we ever experienced a moment of true freedom?
Have we ever experienced freedom from addiction, from
substance, from compulsive relating, from becoming?

In a moment of awakening, of experiencing our innate
wholeness, craving disappears. There is no other thing to
depend on, no other place to go, no other time to covet.
No condition to medicate or escape, no hole to fill. In this
awakening to wholeness is simplicity, the joy of everyday life,
the acceptance of everyday thoughts and feelings. No need to
run, no need to hide, no need to fear, no need to crave.
Simplicity is openness and wonder, simplicity is peace. Peace

is who we are. When we know who we are, we are free: this freedom dissolves the condition that is the root of all cravings, attachments, and dependent identifications.

Leaders must become free of addictions.

The American Dream

"Why are we at Microsoft?" bellowed Microsoft Corp.'s billionaire Executive Vice President Steve Ballmer to a crowd of 9,000 employees packed into the Kingdome, Seattle's indoor stadium. "For the money!" he screamed. "Show me the money!" The crowd responded with a roar: "Show me the money!"

— Los Angeles Times, 12/7/1997

You begin to realize that our economy is based not just on the satisfaction of desire; it's based on the creation of desire. Our economy creates desires; it doesn't just satisfy them. Desires which are created and then satisfied—it's a totally unnatural state of affairs. I was amazed when I realized that this description of our economy was similar to the Buddhist description of samsara, delusion.

— Jacob Needleman

A FEW YEARS AGO, I was asked by the owner and president of a communications company to evaluate the degree to which his company expressed their corporate values in day-to-day activities and interactions.

He asked me if I wanted to review their corporate values documents. I said no. He asked if I would circulate a survey or questionnaire. I said no. He asked if I would use some form of assessment tool. I said no. He asked if I wanted to interview people one-on-one, or in small groups. I said no, I don't want to talk to anyone.

I'm sure he was beginning to think he should have hired another consultant. He asked how I was going to proceed. I said that I was going to use my mute button assessment tool, that I was going to stuff cotton in my ears and then just walk around and watch people work for three days. After that, I would be able to tell him what their actual values were, based on how people conducted themselves in the course of their work. I told him that whatever was printed on his mission, vision, and values document was like pâté, an extravagant indulgence that is served to guests to impress them. I told him it was better to observe what people ate everyday, and so get to know them as they are, not as how they like to think they are. I told him I would rather watch them—without any explanation—to see how they interacted with themselves and each other, with customers, vendors, suppliers, the public, OSHA, the fire department. That is the true values document: how people behave. If people don't like their behavior, they can change. But they have to see how they actually behave: those are their values-in-action, which are the only values worth paying attention to. To superimpose a set of idealized behaviors on top of our actual behavior is a sure way to institutionalize hypocrisy.

I never listen to anyone speak about their values. My ears slam shut and I go deaf. I'd rather watch them. The truth is we are always expressing our values: it is pure nonsense to think that what we say and what we do are two separate things which must be brought into proximity, like two ocean liners coming together, side by side, in the middle of the Atlantic. We might *think* that our real values are what we say they are, but that is a delusional conceit. Our real values are expressed in our actions, in what we do and how we do it. Our actions never contradict our values: our actions *are* our values.

If we believe our values are what we *say* they are, then we will also believe all the reasons and excuses we give about why we don't live up to them. The simple reason we don't live up to our espoused values is that they are not our actual values. "People are our greatest asset" is a popular espoused value of the corporate sector. Though this value is declared, spoken, and repeated by thousands of people every day, we can scarcely see the demonstration of it. It isn't that we fall short because of this devil or that reason, we fall short because we do not value people as our greatest asset.

If we want to know what we value, then we have only to watch what we do and how we do it. If we don't like what we see about ourselves as we observe this, then we can change our behavior.

We don't need to refer to any papers or books or stone tablets for our values. Doing so creates unnecessary tension and anxiety which further obscures what we actually do. We act from what we are, from what is written on the tablet of our hearts. If there is some values work to be done, it is there, in our own hearts. We need to change who we are from the inside out, not because someone else says we should, but because we have looked into the mirror of our actual behavior, and we don't like what we see.

During our first meeting, a company president gave me a bit of the company's history. He outlined their mission, current goals, some personnel problems, and the situation he wanted help with.

I asked him what he valued more than anything else.

He asked for clarification.

I asked him to tell me what he valued more than anything else in life. I asked him to name that single thing which made his life go.

He got up and closed the door to his office. When he sat down, he asked me if I meant at work or in general.

I said there was no difference. There was only life.

After a while, he said that he thought the most important thing in life was love.

I asked him how many people were on his executive team.

He said eight, and that most of them had been with him for about five years.

I remarked that probably all eight of those people knew that love was his most important value.

He said probably not.

I said six.

He said no.

Five?

No.

I asked, "Well, how many of these people with whom you have worked ten hours a day, five days a week, for five years, would know that love is your most important value?"

He hesitated, and then he said, "Probably none."

If that were true, I said, then he was lying about love being his most cherished value, because if it were then everyone would know it.

When I use my mute button values assessment tool on our society, I find that we value the American Dream, an ideal of life based on personal financial success. The American Dream is a dream of getting all the marbles that the visible, material world has to offer. How we do it is not important; what is important is that we get the marbles. If we go through life with no marbles, or only four or five marbles, we will have lost the game of life. If we get all the marbles, or a lot of them, then we will have won the game of life. This is the American Dream.

The American Dream is really the American Nightmare.

The Dream confuses the worth of something in the market place of the visible world with its significance in the invisible world of the soul. The premise of the Dream is based on a misperception about life. The essence of life, its lungs and heart and soul, lie in the invisible, spiritual world. The American Dream is about worth, whereas life is about significance. This is why so many people who have planted their flags on summits of personal achievement and success are still empty, soulless, and desperate. If the worth of something does not originate in the soul's invisible world, it will have no significance, and therefore it will never feed us, it will never fill our hungry bellies.

In 1941, Victor Ganz bought Pablo Picasso's painting *The Dream* for seven thousand dollars. He sold it in 1997 for

48.4 million dollars. The worth of the painting increased unimaginably.

Its worth, however, has nothing to do with significance.

If we look at our society with the mute button on, we can see that we value making money above all else. We love, admire, and celebrate cash cows. Our society demonstrates other values to be sure, but these aren't as dominant as our love of making money. Our inordinate love of money is disconnected from the significance of the invisible world of our soul.

Money can be a servant or a master, a means or an end. In the American Dream, money is the master. Making money has become an end in and of itself, especially in certain industries like the media and sports and entertainment, who profit from our unfortunate addiction to their mostly insignificant products and services.

Leaders will know that money is a means, not an end. Leaders will make money serve the significance of the soul, and will make money serving the true needs of people, not those spurious needs trumped up by their own marketing departments.

The only time I ever saw my elder brother cry was shortly after our father died. Family and friends had gathered at our house to comfort one another. I noticed my brother wander out to the back yard and then slip through the gate into the neighboring park. After a while, I went out and joined him.

He was sitting cross-legged on the dirty grass, head down, sobbing. I don't remember specifically what we spoke of, but I know it had something to do with the deep feelings for life and for those we love which reveal themselves after a great loss. I know that something was said about taking time to smell the roses, about loving, about being present with people instead of living on the freeways of our future hopes and aspirations. I remember rhetorical questions like, "What the hell have I been doing?" Something was said about touching deeper, connecting, feeling, loving, appreciating life itself. I'm sure we spoke of what people everywhere speak of when a father, mother, wife, husband, or child dies suddenly, unexpectedly—and we realize too late that there was something we wanted to say, but didn't; something we wanted to do, but didn't; some way we wanted to be, but weren't. In speaking together after death's rude intrusion, we discover something universal about life, and significance.

Death is a great teacher, which can awaken and enlighten us. Death's teaching power comes from its relationship to life, the cycles of life, the laws of life: everything is impermanent, everything is born, grows, ages, and dies. We don't know if that cycle will last one hour or 100 years or 10,000 years. Death teaches us that we are not in control, that there are greater, invisible forces than us at work in the universe. Death teaches us about now, about this moment, because we realize that it may be our last moment.

Seeing the naked face of our last moment must be like falling into an icy stream; we will come to full attention very quickly. We will forget what is inessential, and remember what is essential. This awakening happens by itself as the cold plunge of death shatters our egoistic delusions. The mystical experience is also an icy stream: plunging into its breathtaking waters shocks us into significance.

I was asked by a client to facilitate his executive team's discussion about corporate values. We agreed to take two days for this, in retreat, off-site.

I proposed that we spend one afternoon on a field trip to a morgue and a cemetery. I thought this would be pertinent to any discussion about values. The president was willing, but the others weren't. They said that if word ever got out, they would be the laughing stock of the company. I couldn't persuade them.

I don't think we can truly evaluate our behavior in the brazen mirror of truth unless we are linked arm in arm with our own death. It is very difficult to live knowingly with the fact of our own death. We might know intellectually that we'll die, but not emotionally. If we don't experience the fact of our own death emotionally, if we don't feel its icy waters, then we will put worth over significance, thinking we have all the time of eternity. We will pursue the American Dream as though we were going to live forever.

One of my clients was the chief financial officer of a project management company. He was twenty-seven years old, married, and the father of an infant son. He was hard on others, impatient and unforgiving. He was even harder on himself. In one of our first meetings, he outlined his plans and goals: he wanted to retire in ten years, with plenty of marbles. That is when he would relax; until then he had to press hard on the grindstone. His wife, who also worked full-time, would bring their son with her to my client's office on Saturdays and Sundays: it was the only way she could see him. They had agreed this was the time to work hard, earn money, and get ahead.

One day I received a call. *Rob, two nights ago I burned myself when I was cooking dinner. Not too badly, but I went to the ER anyway. They took a routine blood test. Today I got the results: I have leukemia.*

His plans changed.

I offered what support I could. I introduced him to relaxation, meditation and visualization techniques, and to the books and tapes of Bernie Siegel, Jerry Jampolsky, and others who speak about the mind/body connection and about the spiritual dimension to healing. We began to speak in depth about things we had only spoken of briefly at the office: values, life and its meaning, plans and their elusiveness, control and surrender, personal will and a higher power. He began to review his life and previous goals in light of these reflections.

At one point during his subsequent chemotherapy, his weight dropped from 255 pounds to about 145. He was six feet four inches tall. At that time, the prognosis was not favorable.

On one of my visits to the hospital, I asked him if he had thought about his death.

A little.

Would you like to speak about that?

Yes.

We didn't speak about death, but about life.

I screwed up. I've been chasing the wrong things. I never took the time to appreciate what I really value.

What do you value?

My wife. My kid. I've hardly noticed them. My God, I value just being alive. I've spent my whole life trying to buy a boat while my life raced by. Now, it might be over and I haven't even lived it.

Today, he owns his own company. I recently worked with him and his company to develop their corporate vision and mission statements and to articulate their operating principles, one of which is: *We are each responsible for maintaining the highest levels of personal well-being—physical, emotional, mental, and spiritual—and for supporting and contributing to the well-being of others.*

Almost ten years ago, I was asked by one of my clients, a corporate president, to design a values retreat for his executive team.

Seven of us set out on horseback and trotted off into the Santa Cruz mountains like urban gunfighters on a mission. We made camp beneath ancient redwoods. The first day we settled in, exhaling the tension and congestion and noise and complexity of the city. I wanted the presence and silence and antiquity of the forest to enter us, individually and as a group, before we started our work.

The next day, we began. I said that any group values statement had to come from individual values statements. If what we, as a group, are going to say is important, then it had better be important to each of us. We can't fake values, I said. I led the seven through a visualization, to get them in touch with the most significant experience they could remember. I thought that would be a good place to begin to speak about what each one valued: go to a valuable experience and mine it.

I asked each person to describe the experience that came to them in the meditation, and what that experience taught them about significance. A vice-president, in his mid-fifties and a former Marine Corps pilot, told of how, when he was 15, he was suddenly transported out of his body. He experienced himself as pure light and was intensely joyful. He felt that he was actually a part of all living things. He said, struggling for the words and with soft tears forming in his eyes, that this light body was the body of everything and that love was the universal spirit of life, binding every living thing together as one. He said he experienced himself as this love, and that he existed everywhere. He said it was an experience thrilling beyond words.

He said it was the most significant experience of his life, though he had not spoken of it for over 40 years. He sat quietly for a bit, and then he said that he didn't feel anyone would understand. He himself didn't understand. There was no support for that experience. He felt it was an anomaly of some kind and thought it best to forget about it. He hadn't known how to build his life from this most significant experience.

In the beginning of this book, I said that mysticism referred to the value of significance. Leaders will know the difference between worth and significance. Leaders will know that money is the servant, the means, of something greater than itself. Leaders will not inflame the unquenchable desires of people for the sake of profit. Leaders will have spoken with their own death, they will be well aware and awake within the eternal invisible world of soul. Leaders will be as strong a teacher as death: leaders will be stern but loving teachers of significance. Leaders will help us calibrate our values-in-action by inflaming our souls, by touching our hearts, and by reminding us of what life is.

Leaders will know that we must awaken from all dreams and nightmares to live in accord with reality. Reality is a leader's value, a leader's fragrance, a leader's behavior. Leaders are prophets of the soul's invisible world of beauty, of love, of joy. Leaders are servants of the soul.

All Things Are Sentient

To the dull mind nature is leaden. To the illumined mind the whole world burns and sparkles with light.

— RALPH WALDO EMERSON

Let it be our weakness, this thirst-love for the world, the sun coming up like red-gold being poured. The potter's wheel moves, and shapes change quickly. Let the jar I am becoming turn to a wine cup. Fill me with your love for being awake.

— HAFIZ

WHEN WE BECOME SENSITIZED TO REALITY, we no longer objectify other living things. We begin to feel their feelings, intuit their language and meanings, understand their rightful place in the world. We come to know that all things are sentient, that "animate" and "inanimate" are false distinctions. We would become very discreet about interfering with, abusing, killing, and destroying living creatures; we would become very careful about polluting and defiling Earth and her lakes and rivers and oceans and her atmosphere. We would, as the

Buddha said, see ourselves in others, and thus cause them no harm.

We do not act as though we know all things are sentient. As it is now, we act as genocidal terrorists who want to purge Earth of her forests, of her plants and animals, strip her of topsoil, pollute every stream, lake, and ocean, defile her air, and push nuclear waste deep into her living center. We do this as though it were our supreme mission in life.

Burning fossil fuels creates 30 billion tons of pollution worldwide in the form of soot and ash, and carbon dioxide and other gases. More than 5.5 billion tons of carbon dioxide are discharged into the air throughout the world every year—about a ton for every person alive. Emissions in the U.S. are currently about 500 times those of developing nations like China and India.

Some 1.2 million barrels of oil are spilled into the Persian Gulf annually.

The Earth loses about 50 million acres a year of rainforests, endangering hundreds of species of trees, plants, mammals, birds, reptiles, amphibians, and insects.

Today, global biological diversity faces a rate of of species destruction greater than at any time since the mass extinctions of the dinosaurs 65 million years ago.

The systematic desecration of Earth and her inhabitants is occurring. We are doing it, or we are allowing it to happen. We are behaving as though someone challenged us, "See if you can make Earth uninhabitable within 50 years. Ready, set, go!" Why are we not ashamed of our behavior?

We can only act in this way if we do not feel the sentience of living things. If we did, we simply could not do what we do. We would feel the pain and suffering of the world's creatures as keenly as we would the mutilation of our own children. In an account on *60 Minutes* of the atrocities in Algeria, a reporter said, "Whole families had their throats cut, men and women were decapitated, babies were tossed into ovens and burned alive, pregnant women were cut open and their fetuses ripped out, and their tiny throats were slit too."

If we can feel this, why can't we feel this for all living creatures?

We have all suffered. We have all experienced pain, fear, loss, hurt. We are grateful to anyone who helps us heal our pain and relieve our suffering. We are grateful to anyone who shows us compassion. We are grateful for the touch of kindness, for the caress of love. Compassion and love elevate our life to the realm of the sacred. Everything is sacred. Everything deserves our respect, our compassion, our love. Everything.

If we could truly feel another's suffering, we would respond with love. No other response is adequate; no other response is appropriate. Finding love within ourselves, we see it everywhere, for we are not different from other living beings and creatures. We are one with them. Their suffering is ours. Their pain is ours. Their fear is ours. Feeling this, we can only respond with compassion, kindness, and love.

Leaders will know that all things are sacred, they will serve all living beings with compassion, kindness, and love.

———

Vivisection is animal experimentation—burning, shocking, drugging, starving, scalding, irradiating, blinding and killing animals. According to PETA, People for the Ethical Treatment of Animals, each year in the United States an estimated 70 million animals are so treated in the name of science, by private institutions, household product and cosmetics companies, government agencies, educational institutions, and scientific centers.

As a society, we have created animal death camps, where millions of animals live in a Dachau or Auschwitz, where they are subjected to horrendous tortures and mutilations. Why can we not hear their unconscionable screams? We cut, stab, splay, flay, starve, irradiate, inflame, poison, and kill millions of animals every year. How is it that we cannot feel their pain and suffering?

Would we bring our young children into these labs? Would we ask our lovely young daughters and sons to come in on a Sunday, perhaps after some religious outing, to sew closed the eyes of monkeys, or to set a pig on fire, or to put solvent on the shaved backs of bunnies? If we don't do this, then why do that? We should only do what we would have our children see.

In order to build and maintain animal death camps, we must stand far outside the heart of living things. The inability to feel the pain, fear, and suffering of animals is the very disease we think we can cure through animal experimentation. The diseases we might hope to cure through vivisection are, themselves, symptoms of the same disease that cannot feel the pain of other living creatures. The disease is soullessness and indifference. If we could cure this disease, a myriad of symptoms would disappear overnight!

Despite the fact that over one million children are neglected and abused in this country every year, despite the persistent torture and killing that exists in almost every country, despite preventable poverty and starvation, we may at least be able to empathize with the suffering of other human beings. It may be harder to empathize with the suffering of insects and animals and trees, of water and air—we may think they are inanimate; we may think they are raw materials which we may use or discard as we wish. We must develop empathy for all living things.

Nothing can be said in the presence of suffering except compassion, nothing can be said in the presence of pain except kindness, nothing can be said in the presence of fear except love. These are the only acceptable responses. When leaders know this, then they will be able to stop what must be stopped. Leaders will know that to inflict pain and suffering, to pollute and defile, to terrorize, torture, and murder is an expression of a single disease: soullessness.

The awakened soul is the great miracle of life. The awakened soul is the great healer. The awakened soul does not cause pain and suffering. The awakened soul does not destroy.

The awakened soul is the lover and the protector of all living things. The awakened soul is the cure for the disease of soul-lessness.

Leaders are awakened souls.

We cannot legislate kindness, compassion, and love. The legislation must come from the inside, as a direct experience of what life is. We must be become a part of the sacredness of life by living in our souls. Our soul is the soul of all, the soul of the world. Our soul knows only one move, one answer, one response, one way: love. Leaders are the embodiment of this love within the soul, and they have only one strategy, one goal, one purpose, one method, one plan: to love and care for all living things.

Leaders will know that all things are living and sentient.

T W E L V E

Pond, Rock, Ripple

Science and religion both teach that we are all interconnected,
and thus interdependent. At the very core, we are all One. But
how do we live as if we know this?

— RAM DASS

If you are a poet, you will see that there is a cloud floating in this
sheet of paper. Without a cloud, there will be no rain; without rain,
the trees cannot grow; and without trees, we cannot make paper. If
we look even more deeply, we can see the sunshine, the logger who
cut the tree, the wheat that became his bread, and his father and
mother. Without all of these things, this sheet of paper cannot exist.
In fact, the entire cosmos is in it—time, space, the earth, the rain,
the minerals in the soil, the sunshine, the cloud, the river, the heat,
the mind. Everything co-exists with this sheet of paper.

— THICH NHAT HANH

WE SHOULD BE VERY THANKFUL to the planet Jupiter, whose
great size and mass produce a gravitational force so strong
that wanton asteroids and meteoroids are sucked into
Jupiter's big mouth, as dustmites into a vacuum cleaner.

Jupiter protects Earth from harm by neutralizing all of these potential catastrophes. Perhaps one or two space rocks get by Jupiter every few hundred thousand years or so, but life on Earth can at least exist and evolve. We are dependent upon Jupiter, although most of us don't know this.

When we open to reality, we understand that everything is related and dependent upon everything else. Nothing lives an independent existence, although we rarely act in accord with this simple fact of existence. Through meditation, self-inquiry, spiritual practice, and mystical insight, the boundaries of our hallucinated separate existence dissolve and we merge into everything that is. This is not metaphorical or symbolic; this is literal. We drink from the same well, we eat from the same table, we breathe the same air, we experience the same joy or pain, love or fear, peace or anger.

More than 250 million years ago, there was only one land mass on Earth, one continent. If we recognize the interdependence of life, we know that time has returned. There are not seven continents, there is one. There are not four oceans, there is one. There are not scores of territorial airspaces, there is only one airspace. There are not myriad seas and lakes and streams, there is only one. There are not many races and religions and nationalities, there is only one.

Because there is only one, everything we think, say, and do is a rock thrown into the pond of our common existence. Whatever ripples are created by our thoughts, words, and actions wash over all of us, equally. We don't readily see this, because we rarely leave the gated community of egoistic living.

Within the sanctum of deep meditation, all differences dissolve. There is only one essence, one consciousness, one heart, one soul. Behind the facade of multiplicity and differences, all things are one thing, and thus all things are related, connected, and mutually dependent.

This mystical insight of interdependence has crucial and pragmatic implications.

Every thought, word, and action is an energetic impulse that moves outward from us in subtler and subtler rippling rings of effect. Unless we are able and willing to see what these effects are, we will continually be victimized by our own shortsightedness. We will wonder at the muddiness of our common well's drinking water. Who did this? Of course, *we* did, but we won't know it. No one would knowingly pour toxic waste upstream, when they know their water supply is downstream. The only way we would do this is if we couldn't recognize the connection between upstream and downstream, between over there and over here, and between you and me.

When driving, we don't keep our eyes locked on the road just in front of the hood of our car. We look farther out and down the road, we look from side to side, and even behind us. We need to take in the whole field in which we drive. We have to have a global awareness that includes ourselves and other drivers, the weather conditions, the speed limit, police hiding behind bushes. We have to be aware of the gas gauge, tire pressure, and the oil light. We have to know where we are in relation to where we are going, we have to notice the road signs and freeway exits. We have to be aware of many things in order to drive safely. We have to take all the information from this global perspective, evaluate it, and act accordingly if we are to have a pleasant trip and arrive safely at our destination. We have to be aware of everything that we do.

The fact that there are more than 40,000 motor vehicle deaths per year in this country makes me wonder if we know how to drive properly, if we have the requisite global awareness to be good drivers.

I wonder if we have the requisite global awareness to *live* properly? Americans consume 8 million barrels of motor and aviation gasoline and gasohol per day, which contributes so heavily to urban pollution and which is so harmful to all living things. Do we know the full story behind this consumption, of the 15 gallons of gas I put in my tank every couple of days? Do we know how this gasoline is made? Where does the oil come from, who profits, and who is exploited? What is the cost to our *common* existence of such consumption? If we don't know the answers to these and other questions, how can we make intelligent choices? If we don't make intelligent, life-affirming choices, aren't we just the sorry victims of our own shortsightedness?

Leaders will be defined by their experience of the interdependence of all things. Leaders will not toss rocks recklessly into the pond of our common existence. They simply cannot.

Power and profit are irresistibly blinding aphrodisiacs. Unless we live from the experienced fact of our interdependence with all of Earth's living creatures and systems, we will not know how to proceed with caution. We will not know how to restrain our impulse toward manifest destiny. We will remain shortsighted and arrogant.

Leaders will live within the context of interdependence. They will live with the knowledge and feeling of the sentience of all living things. Leaders will know how to drive our social and business agendas with the global view that is required for safe living. Leaders will be able to say, "No more dumping upstream!" Leaders will be able to ask the right questions, gather the intelligent data, and act accordingly.

In *Diet For A New America,* John Robbins draws many stunning pictures of the upstream/downstream connection of our choices and actions.

For example, he mentions that in 1985, according to the Meat Importers Council of America, we imported over 100,000 tons of meat from Costa Rica, El Salvador, Guatemala, Honduras, Nicaragua, and Panama. He writes, "To provide pasture for cattle, these countries have been clearing their priceless tropical rainforests." The Meat Importers Council reports that almost all of this meat ends up as fast-food restaurant hamburgers. Mr. Robbins says that in 1960, when the U.S. first began to import beef, Central America had over 130,000 square miles of virgin rainforest, which account for a substantial percentage of the earth's oxygen supplies. In 1985, less than 80,000 square miles remain. At this rate, the entire tropical rainforests of Central America will be gone within 40 years.

Are we enough aware of our interdependence to connect the upstream "I'll have three cheeseburgers" with the downstream destruction of rainforests?

What is the relationship between television and the mental, emotional, and spiritual well-being of our children? Over 35 million TV sets were sold in 1997, with 98% of all households having at least one TV set. There are over 10,500 basic and pay cable TV systems. The 1995-96 average of household TV usage per day was seven hours and seven minutes. In 1996, children between two and five years of age watched an average of 23 hours and 21 minutes of television per week, or about three and a half hours of per day. Children between six and eleven years of age watched an average of 19 hours and 59 minutes per week, over two and three-quarters hours per day.

Mr. Karl Forsyth, who serves on the board of the Aurora Waldorf-Inspired School in Anchorage, wrote the following insightful article about this connection:

Television has become the most pervasive and influential medium in the world today, yet there is abundant evidence that the personal and social costs of our TV habit are far greater than the benefits.

Our culture is TV-saturated, and no longer has the luxury of objectivity on this issue. Still, one can observe in recent history where the first-time introduction of TV into aboriginal cultures was quickly followed by a breakdown in the rituals, activities and thought-processes that evolved over thousands of years, resulting in lethargy, cynicism, social alienation, alcoholism, drug abuse, broken families, suicide, etc.

This is not a coincidence, and if one understands the effect television has on the human psyche, it is not surprising. Our collective and individual imaginations have been supplanted by a relentless and mind-numbing video display. If our future well-being depends on creative people that can draw on a wellspring of inner strength, and I suggest it does, then this loss could be the greatest tragedy of the 20th century.

There are many problems with television, but the most serious are related to the neurological havoc it wreaks in children. It is a drug in every sense of the word, inducing a drowsy semi-hypnotic state of consciousness that kills the creative and thinking processes. For children, this means the impulse for (and the possibility of) creative free play cannot exist while they are watching TV. Yet, the most profound and influential neurological development of a person's life occurs in early childhood during creative free play—literally the future of that child (and of our society) is being formed.

As responsible adults, do we not want each child to fully develop their innate creative, emotional, intellectual and physical capacities? Of course we do. They are a crucial part of the child's development, enabling the young child to work with others, to problem-solve, to picture, to envision, to see inwardly, and respond creatively and positively to life's challenges. These innate capacities develop in the early years during creative, free imaginative play. Yet, we unwittingly over-

whelm and crush this delicate impulse by exposing our children to the constant bombardment of powerful video images. Overwhelming the child's innate imagination in this way results in a reduced and simplified imagination, which in turn reduces and simplifies the development of their neurological pathways, resulting in an actual "dumbing down" of the child.

Our schools are having to deal with a steady supply of 'damaged goods'—in very large part because of extended television watching. The drug-like and damaging effects of the video media are systemic—they cannot be mitigated by "children's programming". Letting our children watch "children's shows" on TV and video is like giving them a vodka martini in a Batman cup. And since the video media kills the young child's impulse for creative free-play, they adopt a passive relationship to the world—outer stimulation and inner emptiness—which makes them at risk for drug and alcohol addiction.

Any systematic and persistent undermining of the critical development processes of a child results in a crippled adult, in some way or other. This systematic crippling process is criminal, because it robs the child-then-adult of potential they may have had at birth, but now will never realize. The worse the assault on the child's full natural development, the greater the tragedy—not just for the child, but for the society that must now compensate in a host of ways for this loss of potential.

For adults, television is just another drug that we should be free to use or not (although it is in our best interest to weigh the hazards). But our children are another matter entirely. We protect our children from a host of "adult" activities: driving, sex, alcohol, gambling, etc. This is as it should be. But we have a gigantic blind spot when it comes to television, which is so much more damaging to children in the long term, that all the other protections we afford are like rearranging the deck chairs on the Titanic. There is something wrong with this picture!

Joseph Chilton Pearce, an expert on human intelligence, creativity and learning, reinforces Mr. Forsyth's view. In his book *Evolution's End,* Mr. Pearce draws upon 20 years of research to show how TV impedes vital neurological development in children. He writes, "As our damaged children grow up and become the parents and teachers, damage will be the norm, the way of life. We will habituate to damage. Nothing else will be known. How can you miss something you can't even recognize, something you never had?"

The following editorial by Jennifer D. Mitchell appeared in the January/February 1998 issue of *World Watch Magazine,* and is another example of the upstream/downstream connection:

If golf wasn't already the world's fastest growing sport, it is now, after the emergence last year of Tiger Woods—a young, charismatic African-Asian-American golfer who won the renowned Masters tournament in 1997. As a result of his rise to fame (heralded by several sponsorships from big names such as Nike), the golf industry is experiencing an increase in the number of participants from New York to Bangkok.

Although Tiger Woods' name—like his profession—may evoke images of wildlife and fields of green, the impact of the growing golf industry is far from environmentally friendly. In effect, wildlife refuges and golf courses are as dissimilar as virgin forests and tree farms—the later being sterile, artificial environments where natural ecosystems and all of their complexities have been compromised.

While Tiger Woods has been able to move mountains as far as racial and demographic barriers are concerned (minorities, women, and children are now the fastest growing segments of the golfing population), his rise is also quite literally moving mountains. In some cases, golf-course developers have lopped 200 feet off a mountain, and moved up to seven million cubic yards of earth—altering, not preserving, natural watersheds. And because the average course requires a minimum of 50 hectares, subsistence farmers, indigenous peoples, and other groups are being pushed off their lands. Each course also requires heavy infusions of pesticides and fertilizers, along with about 3,000 cubic meters of water per day—enough for thousands of city residents. Residents could soon begin to feel the consequences in water-short areas such as Thailand or California.

The president of the U.S. National Golf Foundation has been ecstatic at the possibility that Woods could attract a million new golfers—and their money—to the sport. But to keep up with this surge in new golfers, some 400 golf courses would have to be built in the United States each year. And the new star's agent told Business Week that he "can make a much bigger impact in the Pacific Rim than he has in the U.S." Yet there are already 25 million golfers and 15,930 golf courses in the United States, and another 25 million golfers and only 4,300 courses in the Pacific Rim—where water is scarce, and land is even scarcer.

Much as in Tiger Woods' sudden rise to fame, many of these Asian Tiger economies have ridden an economic boom. Their financial success, however, may prove to be short-lived—an impressive economic surge built on an unsustainable foundation. Similarly, as Tiger Woods drives a new generation toward the sport, golf will increasingly push beyond its sustainable limits. The growing number of golf courses in Asia is already reason for much distress—a symptom perhaps, of the haphazard approach to development that has characterized the region's economies in general. Woods now has the opportunity to help rethink the future of his industry: as the number of golf courses and those lining up to use them grows, the time has come to promote "green" alternatives to traditional greens.

Thoughts and beliefs are self-justifying. We may think and believe that we have the right to do whatever we want. We will always be able to rationalize anything we choose to do, despite any evidence which contradicts our rationale. If we live within the limited context of our ego-identities, we will have no moral, ethical, or spiritual compass to show us the more enlightened path to safe, sane, and harmonious living.

Within the sanctum of deep meditation we find such a compass, which reminds us of our interdependence. We discover that many of our desires are exaggerated expressions of soullessness. We discover that we, in fact, cannot do whatever we want. We discover that there is a universal lawfulness which we must obey, within which we must live and work, with which we must cooperate willingly and happily.

If we can reach the sanctum of silence, we will discover a wholeness of being, and within this wholeness of being we will discover a peace and contentment. Being peaceful and content, our eyes will open to see how every thought, word, and action is a rock thrown into the pond of our common existence.

Leaders will have this compass of silence in their hands at all times.

Don Quixote

There are two ways to be fooled: one is to believe what isn't so,
and the other is to refuse to believe what is so.

— SOREN KIERKEGAARD

DON QUIXOTE IS THE MAIN CHARACTER in a novel written
in the seventeenth century by Miguel de Cervantes. The
hero, Don Quixote, loses his wits from reading too many
romances, and comes to believe that he is a knight destined
to revive the golden age of chivalry. A tall, gaunt man in
armor, he has many comical adventures with his fat squire,
Sancho Panza. Don Quixote's inability to distinguish reality
from the delusions of his imagination finally leads him to
attack a windmill, thinking it is a giant. The giant lives inside
his head, although he sees it outside—in the world, as the
world. Don Quixote doesn't know that his inside is his
outside. He thinks the outside has an independent reality. It's
easy for us to see his mistake. But we don't see our mistake.

　　We too tilt at windmills of delusion, because we don't see
how the outside flows from the inside. We don't see how the
outside world is a picture, a living replica, of our internal pic-

tures. The world is the topography of our mental realm of thoughts and emotions, beliefs, assumptions, opinions, identities, fears, desires, denials: our paradigm. Only when we find our way back to pure awareness will we stop seeing the world as we imagine it is, and begin seeing the world as it actually is.

Why does the world lurch from one sad encounter to another? It is only because we think the external world has an independent reality from our internal consciousness. We think that things *just happen*. We think there are giants, when there are only windmills. In order to see the world as it is, we must first recognize the projected world of our delusions and dismantle them.

One of my clients became Don Quixote in a meeting, tilting his outrage at a giant where none existed. I had worked with him for over a year and knew his background and some salient features of his professional past. I also knew his hot buttons; he had been nicknamed Captain Blast-off by his team, in tribute to his tendency to launch into reactivity—unconscious behavior precipitated by unresolved past emotional experiences—whenever his will was thwarted. I had even bought him a toy rocket ship which he courageously put on his desk to remind him that reactivity, as a state of mind, is the antithesis of awareness.

In this meeting, he was trying to sell his team a particular approach to resolving a manufacturing problem. No one was responding. They didn't believe his data, his analysis, or his recommendations. They questioned him, grilled and challenged him. Captain Blast-off was about to blast-off. I deliberated whether to intervene before or after the launch, and decided after.

His arms were flailing—he looked like Nikita Kruschev pounding his shoe on a table at the United Nations—his head was bobbing forward and back, his face started rippling. I started counting down from ten, silently. I missed only by a few seconds. He launched. He started screaming at his main antagonist, the manufacturing divisional vice president, shrieking the man's name over and over in front of the team, halfway to the moon.

And here is the strange part, the name he was screaming was the name of a former colleague with whom he had had such battles over 20 years ago. The president of a company, with tremendous authority and power to influence the lives of many people, was still jousting with an ancient foe. In that meeting, in that room, at that time, he was Don Quixote charging at the foes in his own head.

Once, a great samurai warrior sought out a Zen master to ask him about a deeper truth than he had ever known, deeper than all his attainments, all his victories, all his renown. He finally came upon the reclusive teacher, and said, "I have heard you know great truths, and I want to know how I can enter the realm of truth, the realm of paradise." The teacher looked at him scornfully, and said, "You? You want to know truth? You seem to me to be a very stupid and arrogant man, who couldn't possibly understand anything other than violence and killing and brute force." At that, the famous warrior became incensed and drew his sword to cut off the teacher's head. "That," said the teacher, pointing to the sword flashing forth from the scabbard, "is hell." The words penetrated to the heart of the samurai, and in an instant of realization, he put the sword back into its sheath. "And that," said the teacher, "is paradise."

By evoking these kinds of confrontations with our conditioned mind, we bring the beliefs of our internal reality into consciousness for scrutiny, making possible a fuller and richer experience of our potential to see how things happen and why.

Are we aware of the images within our mind that cause us to respond in one way or another to what we perceive, or think we perceive?

I've read several studies which establish the number of thoughts we think in a day as 60,000, although the actual number may be greater.

Every 1.44 seconds, we have a thought, which may include emotions: anger, frustration, happiness, sadness, jealously, disappointment. Both thoughts and emotions belong to the mental realm, and these explosive fireworks detonate within us every 1.44 seconds.

How many of these thoughts are we aware of? How many do we notice? How many do we ponder before we act? How many do we question to determine their validity and relevance? How many do we track back to their origin? Until we become acutely aware of each thought and familiar with the place from which they arise, we are victims of our own unconscious reactivity: we can be neither intelligent nor effective, neither creative nor inventive. We will not be able to see what is in front of us.

Imagine driving along Highway 5 in central California, going 75 miles an hour. Every 1.44 seconds your windshield cleaners spurt oil on your windshield. How can you see the road? How can you ever see what is actually there in front of you? This is what happens in us: a darkening and obscuring oil spurt goes off every 1.44 seconds. We cannot see through the oil spurts to where the real world is waiting. We act blindly and stupidly, at the mercy and effect of a process we aren't even aware of.

Our external world is a direct expression of our internal world of thoughts, ideas, and beliefs. In order to transform society, we must first transform ourselves. We must each first investigate our own hearts and minds; we must each discover how we create and project the very things we want to change in the world. The power of awakened consciousness will transform our lives, our institutions and organizations, and society at large. This direct experience of our spiritual con sciousness, free from distortions and conditioning—will show us how to live and work with and from values that affirm life in a sacred and meaningful way.

We must see that the crises in the outer world will never be solved until the crisis in our own consciousness is resolved, because the qualities of our awareness express themselves as our belief systems, which in turn produce our priorities, our values and goals, our attitudes and behavior. We must face directly the attitudes and policies that have fragmented human and ecological relationships, and we must seek deeply within our own hearts for a new vision of compassionate life. The true leaders are those who stand on the frontiers of the spiritual world, shedding the veils of ignorance in order to see that the origin of our difficulties is rooted in the poverty of our awareness.

When the philosopher J. K. Krishnamurti said "the crisis is in our consciousness, not in the world," he alerted all of us to the origin of our actions and the cause of our calamities. If our consciousness is rooted in the fear that shadows a belief in our separateness, then all the world becomes a battleground of self-preservation. If, however, our consciousness is rooted in the mystic perspective of oneness, our motives will be liberated from fear and we will find that we have been immersed in this consciousness from the beginning. Having seen this, having recollected and become conscious of what life is, we will then begin to articulate new patterns for action based on the direct perception of the spiritual reality of which we are a part. This articulation is the province of leaders, whose soothing words steady the dangerously rocking boat of our mind's reckless desires and fears.

We almost automatically attribute our experience of reality to external causes. It is difficult, almost impossible, to recognize that both our experience and our reactions are internally generated and have nothing whatsoever to do with external causes.

What precedes thought? Of what are beliefs made, and how are they formed? What is awareness? What is the mind?

What is beyond the mind? Where do reactions come from? These are questions for leaders.

If we are to ever live with insight and clarity, we must ask these questions. And, we cannot answer them with intellectual answers. We must follow the trail of these questions to their source. We must put on our hiking boots and fill our backpack with food and water; we must find the trailhead and then walk into the wilderness with courage and resolve. Don't bother to take a compass; each person's journey is unique and unprecedented. Each of us must blaze our own trail. Each of us must become intrepid explorers. Each of us must face our own obstacles and adversity. We must develop strength along the way. We must become attentive along the way. We must become transformed by the journey itself.

We will be tempted to stop and set up a camp near some beautiful stream or breathtaking meadow: don't. We might find a startling hilltop view that is too beautiful for words and imparts a deep sense of serenity and calm. Still, don't stop. Keep going deeper and deeper into the wilderness. Follow the trail of experience and reaction to its very source.

When you think you have found it, continue. When you can't continue, continue. When you are lost, continue. When someone else says you have found the source, continue. When you are certain you have gathered the origins of experience and reaction into your own self, continue. Never stop exploring. Never stop wandering. Never stop seeking the source of experience and reaction.

We might want a more precise method or particular instructions then "follow the trail." Are we doing it correctly? Are we making progress? Have we reached the source?

Forget all this, and just begin to follow the trail. The trail itself will be your guide; it will help you.

In 1974, I spent a summer and fall as a mountain guide in the southern Sierra Nevada mountains. In the beginning, I knew nothing. I was a danger to myself and others. I was completely inept. Still, I was hired to escort people into the wilderness on camping trips and on hunting and fishing excursions. I had so much to learn and no time to learn it. People were waiting to be led. Horses were waiting to be saddled. Mules were waiting to be packed. Meals were waiting to be prepared. Emergencies were waiting to be handled. Trail signs were waiting to be read; storms to be weathered; illness and fear and confusion to be mastered.

Who was my teacher, my mentor, my guide? The environment itself. Yes, I did watch and learn from my partner, who had experience in mountain ways. But often I was alone in the backcountry with no guide; I was the guide, and the environment, external and internal, became *my* guide. I was terrified sometimes, other times utterly lost and afraid. One tree looked the same as another. Each rocky trail seemed like the one I had just been on. I thought I was going in circles or crisscrossing back and forth over the same terrain. I had so much to learn.

So, I began. I looked. I listened. I moved with care. I began to discern differences of trees, shrubs, and flowers. I felt weather conditions begin to shift, gather, and disperse. I deciphered the language of sign: animal footprints and droppings; sun and star positions; moon shape and size; horse moods and head, eye, and ear movements. I began to hear rhythms and feel intuitions. I improvised what I needed to know or do in any situation. I became resourceful. I became skillful. The wilderness, which had at first appeared impenetrable, mysterious, and frightening became open, friendly, and majestic.

But I never stopped paying attention. I never stopped learning. I never became arrogant in knowledge or skill. This would have been a disaster. One must always pay attention in the wilderness because it is unpredictable in its very nature. Every moment is new, and one must be ready. Readiness is attention. Attention is vigilance. Vigilance is awareness. Awareness is clarity. Clarity is freedom.

Leaders must take this journey into the wilderness of self-exploration. They must come to know what is within them, the shapes and forms of their conditioned barriers to the radiance of soul. Leaders must exemplify clarity and freedom, and so they must begin to follow the trail of their own experience and reaction to the very source. They must begin now and not stop until they reach the heat of the first fire.

Behind the stream of images and concepts is the field of pure awareness, the uncluttered mind, from which we can see how things happen and why. But when we see and release images and beliefs, it is sometimes painful, as though we die, just a little. We are confronting little tremors of death every time we look at ourselves. Death is but the dissolution of false images of self and the barriers of self-protection we build around them. This process of seeing beneath the surface images of self and beliefs about the world yields powerful gifts: a clear perspective on the origins of things as they appear in our human world, psychological insights about our personal nature and motivations, untangling of confusing and dense emotional states, and revelations of universal proportions—transpersonal glimpses into pure awareness.

Study your own self, not through ideas and philosophies and opinions, not through what you already know, but directly, without images and protection. To study oneself is to examine, to inquire without motive, to see without flinching how one actually lives and thinks and relates. This requires that the deepest parts of our self be drawn out into view. When we have come fully out of hiding, we become vulnerable, and this vulnerability reveals the truth of who we are.

This is the immense task of leadership: to wake up and know which way is north and which way south—this is the work of leaders. To become clear and balanced—this is the work of leaders. To quiet the thunderclouds of anger and fear—this is the work of leaders. To awaken from the slumber of ideas and posturing into the authentic clarity of the real—this is the work of leaders.

Such leaders will pour the abundance of life into the delighted thirsty mouth of the world.

Leadership
Dojos & Zendos

This zendo is not a peaceful haven, but a furnace room for the combustion of our egoistic delusions.

— E I D O R O S H I

IN THE WINTER OF 1969 I cinched up my Aikido *gi* for the first time, bowed, and stepped onto the mat in a small *dojo,* practice hall, in Arcata, California, a little town on the northern coast. The *sensei,* teacher, was a big burly man who looked like a meat packer or longshoreman. Instead, he was a psychologist by profession, and a man of very gentle disposition, although he could throw my ass across the room while barely touching me.

The aikido sensei was also the local Zen master, and I had been sitting zazen, meditation, with him and a small group of students for a few months. I had already had one of the defining moments of my life with him in *dokusan*—a conversation or interview with the teacher—one that continues to reverberate now, even as I type these words. During meditation, the sensei would sit in a small anteroom adjacent to the *zendo,* the meditation room, and await any student who wanted to come and speak with him, perhaps about a koan or some issue of practice, or about anything for that matter. I was studying Zen Buddhism among other subjects at the local college, Humboldt State, and was unknowingly suffering from academic anemia. In the first week of sitting, I decided to go to dokusan. I walked in, turned to close the door, and then sat down on the cushion in front of the sensei. I looked him in the face across our two feet of separation and saw a canyon of impressive features and even more impressive openness.

"Sensei, I wanted to speak with you about zazen. I have been studying at the college and know something of Zen and meditation…"

He leaned forward, just about an inch or two, and asked, "WHAT exactly do you know?"

If he'd fired a cannon ball from his mouth I could not have been hit harder. His question exploded and shredded my face with its shrapnel of clarity. I had never experienced anything like that. I honestly think he had no strategy in his question. He just asked a simple question with such presence and clarity that I incinerated from the blast. It was my first experience with someone who had awakened from the tranquilizing effect of thought overload. The power was enormous. It was as though I had suddenly seen how foolish it was to try and measure the Earth's circumference with a 12-inch ruler. What I thought I knew, and the means by which I knew it, lay in ruins and rubble at my feet.

I remained speechless for a time. I couldn't find my faculties. I had been stripped by a single question. I stared into his face, an abyss of patience waiting for my answer. I had none.

I got up and walked shakily out the door back to my cushion. My nascent interest in truth, freedom, and clarity was solidified in dokusan; I wanted what he had. I quit school shortly afterwards.

Many of the meditators also practiced aikido with sensei, as a way of grounding or integrating meditation experiences and insights into action, into the everyday world. I watched one session and was immediately impressed with the dance-like fluidity of the movements, and the general good humor of the participants towards their art. I signed up.

When watching an adept, aikido may look easy, almost staged. There is whirling and turning and flying and smiling. A video of Morihei Ueshiba, the founder of modern aikido, shows him repel a number of advanced students as they attacked him en masse. All he seemed to do was turn slightly this way or that, maybe duck or twist his hips, maybe extend his arms one way or another; no one touched him and they all just flew through the air and into each other. It looked too simple to be real. I thought that aikido was more of a meditation practice than a useful martial art, like karate or kung fu, and that all the attackers were in some covert way cooperating with the elderly teacher. After all, Mr. Ueshiba had said "The secret of Aikido is to harmonize ourselves with the movement of the universe and bring ourselves into accord with the universe itself. He who has gained the secret of aikido has the universe in himself and can say, 'I am the universe.'"

Soon another cannon shot disabused me of *that* idea. During the first session I tried my hardest to punch a senior student in the mouth. The student disappeared and I went flying. Time after time. Amazing. When it was my turn to be attacked, my awkwardness was stupendous. Had it not been for the compassion of the senior students, I would have been mauled, probably killed. I was so out of sync with the flowing currents they seemed to move in. I was frustrated and impatient, but also inspired. I persevered, not willing to let my clumsiness defeat me. Everyone kept smiling, *Don't worry, keep practicing.*

During each aikido practice, the sensei would work his way around the room to interact with each student at least two or three times. His hands were like ham hocks, except I could hardly feel them when he threw me. I would feel a little pressure, a force of some kind, and then I'd be flying. The odd thing was that whenever the sensei threw me, I'd get up smiling. I think it was a combination of his skill, and of his demonstration of the founder's words *There is no discord in love. There is no enemy of love.* Sensei was demonstrating his love for me, even in conflict situations. Being thrown by him was an exciting and joyful experience. I always smiled. Of course, when it was my turn to practice a technique on him, I felt like a child trying to wrestle an elephant to the ground. It wasn't very exciting or joyful.

I persevered, because I wanted some of what he had and I thought that devoting myself to aikido was the way to get it. I developed a fantasy of one day living in a small back room of a dojo, in which I would teach aikido and meditation. I imagined living in this simple way, deepening my knowledge and oneness with the universe by walking back and forth between my living quarters and my aikido dojo and zazen zendo. I loved the simplicity of the Zen aesthetic; nothing extra, just the essential thing, the thing in itself. I couldn't wait to get my black belt.

Later, I came across Chogyam Trungpa's phrase *spiritual materialism* and realized how easy it is for us to corrupt the pristine, present *presence* with ambition, desire, materialism, possessiveness, and control. I left Arcata about six months after I started practicing aikido, and never again stepped on a mat in earnest. The closest I came to realizing my ambition of being an aikido teacher was in a hepatitis induced hallucination, about four or five years later, in India. In that hallucination, I saw myself living in a small room behind a small dojo. Then I heard a sonic boom of laughter and the picture burst into flames.

Before I left the dojo, I had one tremendous experience. We had been practicing one of the basic techniques for a number of days. It was a technique practiced by all aikido students, regardless of how advanced they become—a wrist throw. A punch to your belly, you step off the line of attack, grasp the attacker's wrist, pivot hips while taking two steps and bringing your second hand to cover the attacker's hand, extend energy. The attacker is supposed to flip and fly and land; then you bring gentle but firm pressure to bear on a wrist lock. They tap out and smile. You smile. Everyone bows. Love prevails.

That's the theory. I never came close, except once, when one evening I threw the sensei; he smiled, I smiled. *Very good* he said. The euphoria was incredible, and it wasn't from pride of achievement, it was from directly experiencing the flow of love and harmony that I sensed sensei experienced. It was what I wanted. I had a lick, a taste, and it was indescribable. *WHAT do you know?* Here, lick this and tell me how it tastes!

I learned much in the zendo and in the dojo during the winter and spring months some 30 years ago as I began the practice of disciplines to cultivate awareness. I began to develop an appreciation for discipline and intensity of effort, and also of surrender and effortlessness. I saw the arrogance and insufficiency of my thoughts and beliefs. I learned about patience, perseverance, humility, and respect. I learned to pay attention, and to appreciate the pain that would always follow when I didn't. If you are present, you can flow; if you are not present, you cannot. Not flowing hurts. I learned about my own ambitions and desires, and about how much I lived in the future. I learned how alive and exciting the body can become when wet with the flow and order and love of creation. I learned how a smile can signify the entrance to the infinite mystery of oneness. I learned that we have to develop our awareness in order to become truly human. I learned of the power of questions, and silence, and clarity, and openness.

I did not learn these things as one learns the multiplication tables; I only began to learn them. I continue to learn them today, although my dojos and zendos are different. But I didn't forget the education of my meditation cushion and of the aikido mat 30 years ago. I took the learning with me when I left, the scar tissue of a cannonball crater shining on my forehead.

A zendo is a meditation room, and a dojo is a martial arts training hall. Whether we use those terms literally or metaphorically, they both refer to specialized environments meant to cultivate awareness, expand consciousness, and teach us to blend with reality: they are places of enlightenment. Leaders will need to visit dojos and zendos on a regular basis. I want to suggest a few that will deepen a leader's contact with reality.

Leadership development in America probably accounts for about a billion of the four billion dollar a year corporate training budget. Most of the expense of that old curriculum will be unnecessary to those who practice and meditate in dojos.

The first dojo is meditation. This is an essential dojo. Leaders meditate. One potent form of meditation is called *vipassana,* or mindfulness meditation. This and other forms of meditation help us to develop awareness, and show us the nature and origin of thought and emotion, of reactivity, of beliefs, of grasping and attachment and fear and desire. Meditation reveals the many dimensions and facets of reality. Meditate every day. Learn to follow the breath into the deep hiding place where it rests, suspended between inhalation and exhalation. There, in the breath's secret lair, is the leader's intelligence.

Silence is another good dojo. Leaders should practice silence, a state of non-dual awareness which grows through the practice of meditation. That silence will come of its own, over time. Until that silence awakens within, practice the silence of not speaking. Do this one day a week, and do it where you work. I don't care if you are the President of the

United States or the CEO of Microsoft. Be quiet one day a week. You will be amazed.

In addition to a daily meditation and a weekly not speaking practice, once a year participate in a weeklong silent meditation retreat. This will unify and strengthen the practice of meditation and not speaking so that the silence of meditation will awaken within you.

Fast one day a week, and one week a year, after visiting your healthcare practitioner to be sure you have no particular ailments that would be exacerbated by this practice. In addition to giving the body much needed rest, fasting shows us how compulsive and unconscious our eating habits are. It helps to bring us awareness of our diet, of our bodies, of emotions that are buried beneath compensatory eating. Fasting also reminds us of the millions of people who live in poverty and who go hungry each day.

Visit the wilderness, live in nature. Live silently and openly and humbly in the deep forests or high mountains or vast deserts. Meditate and fast in silence while living and walking in the wilderness. Leaders must see that nature is not just lumber for our condos and shopping centers, but is a vast storehouse of wisdom and knowledge and beauty and life force. Go on a vision quest under the guidance of a Native American shaman. Live in nature until the urge to pollute and destroy it has left you.

Volunteer to work in a hospice. While caring for those who are actively dying, we may learn much about living. Cradle a dying person in your arms as they pass from this world.

Volunteer as a tutor in an elementary, middle, or high school in your community. Go first to the school whose students are from the poorest families, the most disadvantaged. Do some research, and volunteer in those schools which have the highest incidence of drug use and violence in your city. Listen to the students you tutor as much as you might talk to them. Let their reality penetrate your fantasies. A bumper sticker I noticed three years ago while driving on East Blithedale Avenue in Mill Valley startled me: The Next Time The Air Force Wants To Buy A Bomber, Ask Them To Hold A Bake Sale. Fund Education!

If you are an elected official, whether a state representative or a governor or a senator, a good dojo is the poorest neighborhood of your constituency. For one entire month each year, rent an apartment in the absolutely poorest, most dangerous, drug infested, violently depressed and terrifying area. Live there; work from your home. Don't hide in Sacramento or Washington, D.C. We should demand that all elected officials practice in this dojo; we should make this dojo a requirement of public service.

Be creative in developing your own list of leadership dojos. Think of other dojos in which you can make a strong contact with all aspects of reality: swim with dolphins in order to be tutored by their intelligence. We must all practice the art of leadership; therefore, we must all practice deepening and refining our awareness. We must all make judicious efforts to contact reality. We must all make effort to be accountable for what we do. We must keep lifting our consciousness and opening our hearts: this is the leader's work.

Leaders need to visit dojos and zendos to become impeccably aware. This is their work.

Justifiable Homicide

Any belief system will make a person "set" to notice those events and facts that support their belief and miss those that do not.

— PETER RUSSELL

One may explain water, but the mouth will not become wet. One may expound fully on the nature of fire, but the mouth will not become hot.

— TAKUAN

LIN-CHI, A GREAT ZEN MASTER, once said, "If you meet the Buddha, kill the Buddha." If a great Zen master said it was permissible to kill the Buddha then I feel okay saying if you meet a paradigm, kill the paradigm. *Paradigm* is an au courant term in business. Paradigm and model are often used synonymously, although purists might make sound distinctions.

Paradigms refer to a particular pattern of perceiving reality, created by one's mind, senses, and beliefs. Paradigms are the entire conceptual framework in which we live and through which we perceive the world.

Models refer to the description of a system, organization, theory, or phenomenon that accounts for its properties.

Let's say that paradigms define our reality, and models describe our paradigms, both terms referring to how we create and represent our experience of reality. What I want to say about paradigms is also true of models, so I will use both terms in a loosely equivalent way.

Certain paradigms may be preferable to others. The Dalai Lama travels the world saying that his religion, his paradigm, is kindness and compassion, and he encourages us to live in peace and harmony with ourselves, each other, and with nature. This is a good paradigm. My meditation teacher used to say that the whole world was nothing but the play of the supreme consciousness, that wherever one looked one should see only bits and flecks of consciousness. This is also a good paradigm. These paradigms can be useful to us.

Leaders, however, will need to kill paradigms in order to know reality, just as Lin-Chi said to kill the Buddha in order to become the Buddha. The Buddha who walks around and bumps into you in the street is not the real Buddha of awakened consciousness, but a mere representation of the enlightened state. The Buddha's sermons are not true; they can only point to the truth.

Paradigms and models are mummies stored in the tomb of the mind.

A paradigm is a map, not the land; a menu, not the meal—a mere representation of something which it is not. Leaders, knowers of reality, cannot depend upon paradigms because paradigms lag behind reality. Reality is instantaneous, spontaneous, and non-dual. A paradigm is just the opposite: slow, constructed, and dualistic, a map which is painstakingly drawn to approximate Yosemite Valley, the Himalayas, the Siberian steppes, the Sinai desert.

Paradigms and models are a description of what the mind is and how it works. The mind itself is a pattern of perceiving reality. The mind constructs models of reality: it filters, evaluates, categorizes, names, prioritizes, and organizes. The mind cannot know reality directly, only by inference; the mind can only perceive reality in its rear view mirror.

Leaders must know reality directly. Leaders will not show you maps, they will rub dirt on you. Leaders will not read you menus, they will feed you pecan pie.

Last summer, I was invited to have dinner with three people who were active in personal and organizational transformation and spirituality. That was the topic of our conversation in the very bright and busy Santa Monica restaurant, which served a delicious merlot.

During dinner, each of them spoke about the particular model of transformation which they used in their lecturing and consulting work. I had no model to share.

Every time someone explains how the universe works or demonstrates yet another model of personal transformation I get a ringing in my ears and one part of my brain goes numb while the other starts to ache. I hear what dogs must hear when we speak to them in a reasonable fashion, explaining why they should and shouldn't do something. We think we're being clear and convincing, but they hear *blah blah blah yak yak yak.* The dog thinks, *What the hell is he saying?*

Models are a separating membrane between us and reality, and obscure our seeing. Any model is ultimately antithetical to spiritual insight, to true seeing, which is always spontaneous and intuitive, and shoots like a meteor across the heaven of our mind, disappearing forever in a blazing second. Models are dualistic. They exist within the context of knower and known—the paradigm is the known, and the person is the knower. The knower and the known must come together in knowing, and that knowing is spontaneous and intuitive. Leaders must sacrifice themselves and their models to that knowing.

Many people speak *about* now, *about* being present, *about* the power of intuition and spontaneity, but they don't speak *from* now while *being* present, intuitive, and spontaneous. They speak from the past, from what they have said before, from what they already know. They show maps and read menus.

If we are going to speak about reality, reality should shoot from us like Fourth of July fireworks, booming and exploding, spewing sparks and geysers of light never before seen, never before heard, surprising and delightfully original.

Why don't we trust knowledge to come spontaneously from the well of perfect knowing? Who wants to carry around huge water tanks in their head? Why should we? Wherever we go, there is a well; just drop the cup. Silence is the cup, and we are the well.

It is more important to see who a leader is than what they know. I would like to see leaders who have been struck by lightning, see their split, smoldering, and charred tree trunk of a body. Leaders should hurl shattering reality bolts in our direction, that we may become instantly split apart, and in that smoldering wreckage discover our freedom and essence.

Leaders are free, spontaneous, and original, just like consciousness. Leaders are the presence behind paradigms.

It is so easy to become lazy and inattentive once we've developed a model of how it is, once a pattern has settled like dust on our eyes. We can become secure and complacent with this knowing: there is always a sock drawer for the socks and a t-shirt drawer for the t-shirts. The coats go in the hallway.

How does this knowing come about? How do thoughts grow into beliefs, and beliefs into paradigms? We may need to spend long hours just watching how an experience or a thought becomes a concrete shelter, a gun emplacement on the craggy coastal cliffs of our private country of certainty Should we be content to sit in front of the stage and be amazed by the light and magic show? Shouldn't we want to go behind the curtain to see who the wizard is?

If we want to meet the maker of birds and birdsong, we will have to dump our socks and t-shirts onto the ground and smash our dresser drawers.

People would sometimes come up to me after one of my weekly evening seminars to say how something I had said made perfect sense and had helped them to connect some dots, though they could sense that clarity already fading. They always wanted to know how to remember *it*. They wanted to lock their insight into a paradigm so they could continue to see what they had seen.

I told people to forget about remembering. What was important was not what they had seen, but the ability to *see*. Seeing results from emptying oneself of everything, and then throwing away the empty self, so that the moment itself lives through us. Marry the moment, love the moment, become the moment. The moment is always poignant, which is why so many were so affected, and the moment is also fleeting, which is why no one could remember.

To those who persisted with *how to remember,* I said live as Gale Sayers ran with the football. Never before, never again, always spontaneous: he improvised moves from now, in now, seeing where to go and what to do and how to do it now, not before or later, but now. See.

I walked into the office of a client, a project director for a construction management company. He had forgotten about our meeting, even though I had flown from San Francisco to Boston at his request.

"Well, anyway, it's a good thing you're here. I feel like my 94-year-old grandfather. Every time I visit him, he looks at me and pleads, 'Just tell me where I am!' That's how I feel. I'm so buried with this project, I don't even know where

I am." He couldn't see anything except the shadows of his own anxiety and confusion. His every action was aimed at these shadows and produced only an escalation of tension and helplessness within the office.

We must all learn to *see* clearly what is actually happening and be able to discern the difference between what is real and what is imaginary.

Most people don't see well, if at all. It's understandable: we never learned how. Anais Nin wrote, "We don't see things as they are, we see them as we are." Isn't this true? We usually see only our own thoughts and feelings *about* what we imagine is happening superimposed on what *actually* is happening.

So, how does one see more clearly, more realistically? Our first response is to do something, to learn something new. We can find numerous techniques, strategies, and philosophies in the plethora of self-improvement books, audio- and videotape programs, and seminars currently available. We may be tempted to exchange our current paradigm for a new paradigm, thinking that this will help us *see* better.

My advice is: If you see a new paradigm, kill it. It will only make things worse.

In order to see, we must be free from patterns, because a pattern—any pattern—is another projection of our mind onto what we are trying to see. More shadows, less light.

My response to my client's state—as it is with almost all situations asking for clarity, problems asking for solutions, doubts asking for assurance—was to request that he sit quietly, relax, attend to his breathing and let silence suffuse his whole being. I requested that he not think differently or change anything, but that he become more aware by becoming silent.

Awareness cannot be adequately defined because it cannot be objectified. It refers to a unified field of consciousness, a field of pure awareness so vast and untrammeled that all things are contained within it. This unified field is awareness itself. Awareness is a direct seeing into the moment, without projection; it is clear insight. Awareness is a light that illuminates all situations and objects and thoughts. Awareness is the eye that sees things as they are, not as we would like them to be, or hope they are, or imagine they are. Awareness is the eye that sees motive, intent, cause, and solution. When one sees with the eye of awareness, appropriate and correct action arises spontaneously out of the situation itself.

In order to see things as they are, we must develop clear awareness. This means that we do not pile our fantasies onto a situation. In order not to add our distorting projections, we must internally free ourself from images, opinions, beliefs, and interests in outcomes or results. These are all obstructions to clarity. When we dissolve these internal structures of patterned perceiving, awareness itself remains.

We can only see deeply into the pond of the mind if the sediment of thoughts and images has settled through meditation and silence. When our internal structures of patterned perceiving collapse in silence, awareness itself grows like a lovely lotus above the mud. The philosopher J. K. Krishnamurti said, "Silence comes when thought has understood its own beginning, its own nature, and how all thought is never free but always old. To see all this, to see the movement of every thought, to understand it, to be aware of it, is to come to the silence which is meditation."

Awareness itself, not representational paradigms and mechanical models, is the means of seeing, of perceiving, what is happening in reality. Awareness is not distorted by first, second, or third thoughts; or by anxiety, doubt, or self-interest. Awareness does not turn away in denial, does not grab with desire. Awareness is simple, quiet, present. Awareness *means* "what is."

The great sage Ramana Maharshi said, "Effortless and choiceless awareness is our real state." Entering into our real state will always illuminate who we are, where we are, and what we are doing. In this way, we will always know what to do and how to do it. We will not become lost in labyrinths of anxiety, doubt, fear, and confusion. We will not need to act rashly from fear or inelegantly from anxiety and confusion. Awareness itself is enough, it is an engine of enormous power.

The publisher of a business newsletter asked people to submit for publication articles that "pushed the envelope." This is a familiar phrase, often used in executive planning meetings and team building sessions. I think the phrase was coined by the celebrated pilot Chuck Yeager, who was suggesting that by pushing the edges of the envelope, we would stretch the boundaries of the known and, therefore, the possible. We might say that the envelope is our world view, our paradigm. If we are to learn and grow, if we are to actualize our human potential, we must push out from what we

already know; we must expand the playing field of our perceptions. It strikes me that there are different kinds of
envelopes.

One envelope would be that of performance and achievement, of compelling concern and interest to business people.
If we are not pushing out the frontiers of what we know
about ourselves and our capacities, we will be stuck in an
endless repetition of what we have already done. There is no
creativity, no innovation, no burst of inspiration or brilliance
without this pushing. Corporate America spends more
than four billion dollars a year on training and education
programs and products, all of which, in one way or another,
are intended to facilitate people's process of pushing the
envelope.

We might address another envelope with the word
"relationship." Pushing on this envelope will result in a more
astute understanding of intra- and interpersonal dynamics
and occurrences. This, in turn, would lead to clarity about
oneself and to skillful and generous responses to others.
Pushing harder on this envelope would bring insight about
our place in the ecology of living systems and would probably
inspire an empathetic, perhaps compassionate, resonance
with everything that is alive on this planet. The more we
expand, the more we will see our personal and corporate
responsibility to the whole of the living world, not just to
the part of it with which we are most identified.

There is also the somewhat abstract envelope of values,
and we certainly want to push here. In this regard, we must
investigate the origins and validity of our values. We need to
spend a lot of time refining our values as we explore truth

and consciousness. After all, our values define our commitments, our commitments define our actions, and our actions affect everyone, so shouldn't we refer to our values at least as often as we do the stock quotes?

In the realm of being, we can also push the edges of the envelope. In this context, we redefine our knowledge of reality and transform our experience of self. In this envelope, we encounter our own minds and hearts, their qualities and content. This is where we see who and what we are. Again, if we are to be explorers and test pilots for the miraculous, the mysterious, if we are to cross the thought-to-be-impenetrable boundaries of being, we must not be satisfied with what we already know, regardless of how certain we are. Not long ago, experts were certain that no one could run a four-minute mile. Today, doing so is commonplace. We hold many incorrect ideas about the nature of being, so we ought to push this envelope. We should bring the heavy equipment and dig deep, unearth ancient signs of unseen civilizations living within us.

Using these examples, we start within the envelope of our current paradigm and push out. We push, extend the boundaries, expand the possibilities, change the paradigm, and then we use the new one, until we exchange it for another. We are still prisoners of representation and rear-view mirror reality.

Leaders will know of another pushing force, one we may have to take a poetic leap to appreciate. Sometimes, something from outside the envelope pushes on us. When this happens, our envelope—no matter how big and stretched—disintegrates as a spacecraft without a heat shield would upon reentering the Earth's atmosphere. We land on real earth, eating real food.

When our envelope, our self-concept and world view, disintegrates, we disintegrate also. We are suddenly without an envelope, everywhere at once, being nowhere in particular.

Before he disappeared into the clouds, Lao Tzu wrote, "Knowledge creates doubt, and doubt makes you ravenous for more knowledge. You can't get full eating this way. The wise person dines on something more subtle: He eats the understanding that the named was born from the unnamed, that all being flows from non-being, that the describable world emanates from an indescribable source. He finds this subtle truth inside his own self, and becomes completely content."

The movie *Shine* portrays a young pianist named David Helfgott who wants to perform Rachmaninoff's Piano Concerto No. 3 in D Minor. At first his mentor tries to dissuade him. He says that no one so young would be mad enough to attempt to play the piece; it is too dangerous. David says he is mad enough to try. His teacher relents, and tells him that he will have to learn every note as it is on the page. He will have to play it blindfolded. And then, only then, he will have to forget them. He has to learn the notes, then forget them; then the music can be played. He has to learn the pattern, and then go beyond the pattern.

He practices and practices the pattern. His fingers become demons of speed and agility. His practice carves new routes of responsiveness in his brain. He is told to be bold in his attack. He attacks with single-minded focus. He learns the notes and the piano shakes. He grows in his madness.

One day, the piano strings break under the boldness of his attack. The teacher says with a broad smile, "Ah, now we're getting somewhere." Then comes the day of the performance. It is stunning. The notes are forgotten in the furious play.

How could *that* playing be contained in the notes? It is not possible. That stunning fury of beauty and power could only come through impeccably empty canyons. The emptiness is what practicing the notes with boldness left behind when the piano strings broke. There was only music.

My teacher used to talk about the goal of mantra meditation as being the union of mantra, its meaning, and the meditator. That's all he would really say. It never hit me with any force during all the times I heard him say it. When I saw the piano strings break and the furious play that came in the aftermath, I understood. When the notes, the music it represents, and the player become a single creative force, then the true music just pounds through consciousness with a fury of enchantment beyond description. One day, as we practice what our teachers tell us to practice, our piano strings will break. This means we have carved enough emptiness in ourselves to allow the furious play of true living. True living will have claimed us. From then on, we cannot practice; we can only live. When the piano strings break, we break into canyons of emptiness.

When we become lovers of enchantment, the further work is to love the music, to be taken over and over by it in fits of love-making. Do not let the mind enter. Do not let the practice enter. Let all that go; do not fix the piano strings. The music played on a piano with no strings is the music of a leader.

The leader is a wine of freedom and love, aging and ripening to perfection in this cask of canyons booming with silence.

Mentored By Carrots

*Only awareness, which has nothing to do with mental activity,
which is free from all reference to the past, free from bodily and
psychological habits, free from selection and repetition, can open
the door to spontaneous understanding.*

    — J E A N   K L E I N

*If you use your mind to study reality, you won't understand either
your mind or reality. If you study reality without using your mind,
you'll understand both.*

    — B O D H I D H A R M A

IN GREEK MYTHOLOGY, Mentor was the trusted counselor of
Odysseus, and the word has come to mean wise and trusted
counselor. This notion of a mentor is described and recom-
mended in many books on management and leadership, and
is gaining currency in professional training programs. In professional circles, it is thought to be a good idea to have a
mentor to teach one new skills, to refine one's attitudes and
behaviors, and to guide one's career, especially as one enters
the upper echelons of an organization. There, as one begins

to enter the narrowing and competitive world of executive advancement, the mentoring becomes increasingly political.

A mentor is a good thing to have. One of my early mentors taught me something that revolutionized my life: the difference between thought and awareness. My mentor taught me how to pay attention. As my ability to pay attention deepened, I came into the awareness of things as they are, of life as it is. I learned that without this awareness of things as they are, we are asleep and dreaming. Leadership must be rooted in awareness, not in sleep and dreams.

What I learned is the very essence of mysticism. I learned that thoughts and beliefs—which are cults of like-minded thought clusters—obscure reality. Reality itself is between and behind thoughts. I learned that each thought is its own advocate, which is why we can rationalize or justify anything, even the crudest and most horrific behavior, because the thoughts behind the behavior are self-justifying. I learned that conceptual thinking, being self-justifying, cannot admit the consequences of its own actions, it cannot make connections of accountability because it only justifies.

I was reminded of this by an article in the *Los Angeles Times* on February 22, 1998, about pilots aboard the aircraft carrier U.S.S. George Washington and their readiness for an air attack against Iraq. Lt. Reuel Sample, the ship's chaplain, said, "Do they worry about hitting civilians? Yes, they do. But to be perfectly honest, in order for them to get their job done, they need to put that out of their minds...We as Christians strive for peace, but sometimes God uses war to bring about peace." Does God need to use war to bring about peace? Would God ask anyone to put killing people out of their minds?

God has nothing to do with this. Thoughts and beliefs and their actions are self-justifying, especially those concepts with which we sincerely and seriously link our sense of self, our ego—concepts that define who we think we are—such as concepts of national and religious affiliation and identity. Blaise Pascal, the French scientist and philosopher, vivifies this with words written three hundred years ago: "Men never do evil so completely and cheerfully as when they do it from religious conviction."

Living within the abstract identities of the ego, we cannot see what we do, we can only see our justifications. We will justify any behavior that serves our beliefs and our identities. In order to live intelligently and harmoniously with each other and with nature, we have to see the limitations and self-justifying characteristics of thoughts and beliefs. We have to develop a desire for truth, not justification. We have to become hungry for truth, and sick of rationalization.

Loyalty to the ego and its beliefs is the root reason behind tragic behavior by individuals and organizations; it is the cause of corporate pollution and governmental abuse of power. It is why CIA operatives might traffic in drugs, because their loyalty, their allegiance, is to some kind of Oliver Northian patriotism, or some other abstract identity which is used to justify their behavior. They are not committed to the truth. It is why tobacco industry executives might lie, en masse, to an incredulous American public—their loyalty is to personal and corporate profitability, not to truth.

Leaders must be loyal to truth.

Conceptual thinking is the body of the ego, our sense of individuality. We are nothing but clusters of thoughts and ideas and patterns of identity. When a thought, an idea, a concept, or a belief is challenged, threatened, or imperiled, the ego responds as though its own life were threatened or imperiled. In order to see who we truly are, in order to be able and willing to be accountable for our actions in the world, we need to die to conceptual thinking and become resurrected in awareness.

This is what Nisargadatta Maharaj meant when he said, "Do not be afraid of freedom from desire and fear. It enables you to live a life so different from all you know, so much more interesting and intense, that, truly, by losing all, you gain all."

We have to be exceedingly mindful about those thoughts and ideas with which we identify; they become a description of our self-image, they become *who we think we are,* while who we actually are is forgotten. The strong trunk of identity upon which grows branches and leaves and flowers of lesser identities is obsessive-compulsive egoism—a mental tic that obscures reality. If we cannot see or know reality, we cannot act in accord with it. We take our orders from the willfulness of this mental tic of egoism.

We will defend this trunk of egoism and this tree of identities to the death—to the death—against any and all real or imagined threats and assaults. Our survival becomes the survival of our identities. We will deny, discredit, or destroy everything that threatens the survival of our identities. It can be difficult to recognize and name our identities because they may be so barricaded behind impenetrable walls of emotional and psychological defenses; but we can certainly recognize their affect: arrogance, vanity, and conceit, which are the motives for every act of abuse and defilement against life and her family of living creatures.

We can see the wreckage of this reckless behavior everywhere we care to look. We can, for example, see it in the climactic changes in Earth's atmosphere as a result of an industrial behemoth whose products feed our extravagant lifestyle and whose waste streams are the unpayable bill. In the introduction to his book *The Heat Is On: The High-Stakes Battle Over Earth's Threatened Climate,* Ross Gelbspan writes, "The reason that most Americans don't know what is happening to the climate is that the oil and coal industries have spent millions of dollars to persuade them that global warming isn't happening."

Of course, we have to ask if we really want to know. We may not, because knowing what is actually happening might be too threatening to our identities. We may choose to deny what is happening in the world with the magic wands of arrogance, vanity, and conceit.

———

The mentor which taught me about awareness was a pile of carrots.

I lived for four years in an ashram, a meditation center, in India, during which time I was assigned a variety of chores as part of the daily routine. One day, I was asked to work in the kitchen. All the food was cleaned, cut, and prepared by hand.

I was asked to become a vegetable chopper. Fine, happy to do it. That is when and how I met my mentor. While I also learned from eggplants and tomatoes and potatoes, the carrot was the superior teacher.

I was shown how to hold the knife, how to stand properly, and how to slice each carrot into precisely angled pieces of a certain thickness. This was important; each slice had to be according to specification—a precise angle and thickness.

Each morning at about 4:00 a.m., I would go to the kitchen to be tortured by the carrots. Every task in an ashram serves a dual purpose. The first is to do the thing itself, to chop vegetables, to sweep a path, to care for a horse or cow. In this regard, it was a job that you were to do as well as you could. The second purpose of any task in an ashram is to mirror your level of attention, so that you can become more proficient in awareness. This second aspect of any task brings the thing at hand into the realm of meditation. Everything in an ashram is a meditation; each and every instant is a means of increasing awareness. That is any ashram's purpose for being: to increase awareness through direct experience of reality.

In the beginning of one's curriculum of task-as-meditation, the teacher, or some senior students, would become the helper of the task. They would point out when the students were not paying attention. The supervisor of the vegetable choppers would watch me with fierce and unforgiving eyes. If my posture wobbled, she yelled at me. If my grip on the knife weakened, if I looked up and around at others, she scolded me. The worst always came when I stared off into space, hallucinating imaginary events. I'd usually be brought back into the present by a potato thud against my head. The supervisor was supposed to do that. It was her job to help me become aware.

The most ruthless teachers of all, though, were the carrot slices themselves. I had been shown what to do and how to do it. Each slice had to be just so: a certain angle and thickness. Knife thrust after knife thrust, slice after slice, carrot after carrot, day after day, week after week. Each slice just so. I don't know that anyone who ate what we prepared with the carrots was particularly interested in the just so-ness of each slice. That wasn't the point. Becoming aware was the point. I lived in that particular realm of carrot mentoring for about three months.

The supervisor's greatest joy was in rummaging through my mounds of slices, looking for one that was not just so. For the first few weeks after I started, this was easy. I rarely, if ever, made a cut just so. After a time, I hit the mark maybe one in three, which would have been a good average in baseball. Not here. Somewhere around carrot number 30,000, I began paying attention. My batting average was up to around .800. My posture, grip, and cutting motion were all solid. I didn't look around. I didn't stare into space. I was right there, about 80% of the time. Better, good even; but not good enough. We were expected to bat a thousand, no excuses.

And why not? We had an unambiguous assignment, raw materials, the tools, the training, the ability. With nothing missing, what's the problem, what's the variable? Attention. It was always and only attention. Paying attention. I can now, 25 years later, hear my supervisor screaming and spluttering in my face: *Pay attention! Concentrate! Focus!*

Bat a thousand? Why not? What's in the way? I learned that the only distraction to batting a thousand is the quality of our awareness, the clarity of our attention to now, to what we are doing, to what is happening. Even our technique is a function of awareness. This is the great teaching of the carrots: pay attention.

The carrots also showed me why I couldn't pay attention: I was lost in my thoughts, without even knowing it. This was what compromised and corrupted clear attention every time: being lost in thought without even knowing it.

A visitor once asked a New Yorker how to get to Carnegie Hall. "Practice, practice, practice" was the answer. So it is with becoming aware. We practice awareness by paying attention to what we are doing, and noticing what happens within ourself when we stop paying attention, when we slice the carrots out of spec; when we cut our finger; when a potato thuds against our head, causing us to jump and awaken, startled and embarrassed.

What happens is that our attention leaps on the back of a thought and rides off into the sunset, leaving the carrots behind, without our noticing. Just as we have to pay attention to what we are doing on the outside, we have to also pay attention to what we are doing on the inside. We lose our awareness, our capacity to pay attention to what is, when, instead of noticing our thoughts and feelings, we become them. This is when we will cut our finger, or worse. If we are running a billion dollar multinational company, or leading a country, losing our awareness to rampaging thoughts and strong emotional tides will be disastrous.

We might think there are variables other than the quality of awareness which would keep us from batting .1000. Motivation. Desire. Commitment. Loyalty. Incentive. Purpose. Meaning. These are all issues with which we struggle daily; and these are also the daily concerns of leaders charged with vivifying their organizations to excite morale and performance. These are never a problem if one is paying attention.

In the ashram, there were a few ironclad rules. One was that we had to show up for everything, everyday, whether it was meditation, chanting sacred texts, working, studying, washing clothes, listening to lectures; whatever. *Show up or be gone.* If we were too sick to show up, we had to leave the ashram in order to get well. There was no middle ground. Show up or be gone, that was the fundamental, nonnegotiable, unbreakable rule.

There were days when I didn't have the motivation or desire to go to the kitchen. Some days I was ill. I wanted to sleep in. I wanted a more interesting job. I was pissed at the supervisor, or the teacher, or the monsoon season, or the infection in my leg or parasites in my belly. Show up or be gone. I showed up. In showing up, I noticed that motivation, desire, commitment, incentive, meaning, purpose—were just movements of the mind. As long as we live lost and sleeping in our thoughts, these thoughts will trouble us, and intrude upon our stillness and efficiency of living with insatiable demands. When awareness co-opts our thoughtstream, we are motivated and moved by an implacable force which needs no manipulation or coercion to fulfill itself.

This constant paying attention to what we are doing, which includes what we are doing inside ourselves, allows awareness, or consciousness, to emerge, unfold, and expand. It is a second sight, bigger and more encompassing and accurate than our thoughts, hallucinations, and rampant, unrestrained reactions—all of the distractions to awareness we notice for ourselves while practicing paying attention. Awareness is not localized in our brains and dependent upon our senses; it is the actual presence of the animating life force, the supreme creative power of the universe, set free within our own self.

As I became more adept at paying attention, I began to bat consistently at around .900. Sometimes, for a few minutes, I could bat .1000. During one of these hot streaks, the supervisor, try as she might, had to let handfuls of carrot slices pour through her fingers without comment. She looked at me. I looked at her. She was not impressed. I was not proud. It was just so. Here, cut these carrots at this angle and at this thickness. Fine. Done.

Through this training, I learned how to pay attention to what I was doing, and I could notice much of what was going on inside my body and mind. I had noticed that awareness was behind and around all of this, even marbled through it. I might still go to sleep, but I was able to notice it, almost immediately. As a result, whatever I was doing, I did well, very well. I had become an artisan in life, just by paying attention. It was a time of lucidity. I suppose this was progress.

Then, something finer happened.

Up to that point, my practice field was the carrot piles in front of me, my task, and my thoughts and feelings. One day, a 20 dollar wall clock expanded the playing field. I had never noticed it before, it was too remote from where I was paying attention. Then I heard it tick and tock, tick and tock. I had never *heard* it before. Now I did. My practice field just got bigger. Spontaneously, I began to notice more and more, farther and farther afield. I could hear people breathe, feel drawers open silently, sense pots being lifted out of sight. This is when the concentration and focus of paying attention—noticing what I was doing and what was happening around and within me—was catalyzed by awareness and exploded into something I had not experienced before except in deep, eyes-closed, seated meditation.

I was suddenly alive and awake in a field of consciousness, in which I had clear focus and perception of what was at hand—including the thoughts being dealt like cards from my mind and the commuter struggles of blood corpuscles in my arteries—and the simultaneous sensual or intuitive perception of a larger field that could include two people speaking 50 yards away, a lizard sunning on a rock an hour's bus ride away, or smoothly-curved arcs of glowing celestial blue matter, 20 million billion miles long, drifting orca-like between galaxies in deep space.

The conceptual self dies in all of this, but is resurrected by it, too; one's new life is in all things, everywhere, resurrected, wild and holy, unique but never separate. One's mind is the very mind of life. One is too full to want, too secure to doubt, to serene to fear. In the galaxy of our life, we move orca-like, gentle, simple, trusting, loving.

Paying attention until awareness lifts us out of conceptual thinking is meditation. Meditation is awareness, and awareness enfolds all of life. Leaders must know this.

A significant number of school age children—perhaps as many as 8%—have Attention Deficit Disorder, or ADD. Doctors and educators often use the term to describe the way certain children act in the classroom. These children have difficulty learning in school, paying attention and behaving. They squirm in their seats, fiddle with their papers, fidget with their hands, and move around to such an extent that they disturb other children. They raise their hands frequently and answer questions even if they don't know the answer. Their activity, questions, noise-making, and general busyness can be irritating to the teacher and other students alike. This disorder is also called Attention Deficit Hyperactivity Disorder, ADHD.

Many parents report that these children have had their problems since they were babies. As toddlers, they were always climbing, breaking things, throwing objects around the house, climbing out of their cribs and generally getting into mischief.

The cause of ADHD remains unknown. Environmental factors, including parenting techniques, diet, and toxins appear to affect the disorder, but they do not cause it. Some scientists think there may be a chemical imbalance in these children; biochemical interactions related to the brain's neurotransmitters, especially the dopamine and serotonin pathways, are involved. Prenatal risks and birth complications may be implicated in some cases. Some doctors think that hyperactivity or the attention-deficit problem may be an inherited illness, much in the way that hypertension or diabetes runs in families.

The core symptoms of ADHD are inattention, impulsivity, and hyperactivity. In children, these symptoms manifest themselves in different ways, including:

- failing to give close attention to details or making careless mistakes
- difficulty sustaining attention
- appearing not to listen when spoken to directly
- not following through on instructions and failing to complete tasks
- organizational difficulties
- avoiding, or not liking, tasks that require sustained mental effort
- losing things necessary for tasks
- being easily distracted
- forgetfulness
- fidgeting
- inability to remain seated when necessary
- feelings of restlessness or excessive activity
- difficulty engaging in leisure activities quietly
- feeling as if "driven by a motor"
- talking excessively
- blurting out answers before questions have been completed
- impatience—or difficulty waiting
- interrupting others in activities or conversation.

By adulthood, individuals may show other signs in addition to the above symptom list. These include:

- poor organization
- rapidly shifting moods
- hot temper
- over-sensitivity
- low frustration tolerance
- physical hyperarousal
- over-reactivity
- emotional hyperarousal
- forgetfulness
- low ability to plan ahead
- depression
- low self-esteem
- relationship difficulties
- feelings of inadequacy
- poor financial management
- poor time management
- career uncertainty
- impulse buying
- accident proneness
- academic underachievement
- numerous job changes
- difficulty paying bills
- alcohol or drug abuse
- difficulty sleeping
- feelings of disappointment or guilt.

When I read these lists of symptoms, I realized that almost every executive I have ever met or worked with has ADHD.

Almost every person in America has ADHD. Perhaps not every executive and person in America has "clinical" ADHD, The statement is metaphorical. In this metaphor, it is not the teacher and other students who are disturbed by the ADHD behavior; it is the order and lawfulness of life itself. It is one thing when a nine-year-old boy explodes in his classroom; it is another thing when a 62-year-old President does the same thing, but has tanks and aircraft carriers and fighter-bombers at his disposal.

The ADHD I am speaking of is a disorder of consciousness, of awareness. We are unable to see and know reality, because we cannot sit still long enough to let the onslaught of our thoughts and feelings fade to calm awareness. We cannot follow the instructions of reality because it is too subtle for our hyperactive physical, mental, and emotional selves. We cannot live harmoniously with others and with our environment because our frustrations erupt in destructive tantrums. We remain, in spite of the evidence, unaccountable for the results of our actions because we are too compulsively kinetic and inattentive to add two and two: we come up with sixteen. When we have this disorder, we disrupt the world in far more serious ways than a child disrupts the classroom; we disrupt the balance of nature and throw everything into disorder and disarray. To know reality and to serve reality requires stillness, subtlety, and attention, which are the symptoms of awareness, the antidote to ADHD.

The treatment for ADHD is meditation. Leaders must meditate. It is the only means to cure the hyperactivity of this type of ADHD. Meditation will cure this condition.

At first, meditation is a practice that teaches us to focus our attention on a single point, perhaps the breath or a mantra or the space between two thoughts. As we focus, we are amazed to discover how many thoughts we have. We begin to see that the mind is nothing but thoughts about things, and thoughts about thoughts. We can observe the chaos of the mind, racing without order or purpose from one thing to the next, careening from the past to the future while barely touching the present moment. We also see that all of these thoughts are self-centered; our whole internal experience is qualified by a central thought, the image of "me."

As we continue to focus the mind, we begin to observe our thoughts and feeling states without getting lost in them. We see that these mental/emotional states arise in number-less waves within the mind. That which observes the play of thoughts is not the mind but the awareness from which the mind itself is born. We can see that this awareness is qualita-tively different than thinking. It has a depth and silence to it. Gradually, we begin to perceive through this awareness, in silence, without thoughts, images and symbols. And, as we do, our own sense of self becomes transparent.

Meditation ends the anxiety of self-centeredness because it invites us into the silence of pure awareness. In this aware-ness, our spirit is liberated from conditions. We no longer need strategies in life, because the fundamental condition that needs strategies—the condition of "me"—has disap-peared.

Our entry into this silence marks the end of meditation as a practice and the beginning of meditation as a state of being.

Our chronic restlessness subsides. A different way of seeing and knowing is aroused, a capacity of intuitive perception that is wholistic and instantaneous.

In the stillness, we feel a subtle, pervasive presence. When we try to know that presence, it recedes, returning as we relax and simply allow it to be. Our thoughts and struggles appear in the midst of all of this, but they no longer obscure that presence. This is called natural meditation. It is the encounter with our Source. It is who we are, once we have relinquished our smallness, pettiness, and fear. As we relax into awareness, we see that we are the background from which all these forms arise. We see this glowing presence as a shimmering light around everything. It is indescribably beautiful and in the midst of this beauty we fall in love with all things.

Meditation is an ending of ourselves and an opening into the life-stream which flows invisibly behind the visible world of forms—a flow of beauty, peace, and love. We've forgotten about the Invisible Source; nonetheless, it is the very ground upon which we stand. It is the essence of what we are, though we constantly overlook its shattering simplicity and ever-presence. We can never be fulfilled unless we return to our Source.

Whether we see it nor not, the light of the invisible Source shines within us. If we would just sit quietly by the open window of our heart for a few minutes each day, soon that light would be evident to us, and soon that awakened light would heal, inspire, and enlighten us. We would enter reality, knowingly, and become lovers and servants of this reality.

If we need an image of that light within us for the sake
of the mind that becomes lost in its brilliance, we might see
a single white rose glistening in the early morning sun,
growing towards eternity.

Beyond Peace

Why are you unhappy? Because 98.99% of everything you do and all that you say is for yourself, and you don't have one.

— Wu Wei

The essential knowledge must be attained by everyone. What is this essential knowledge? For the individual self to know the mystery of the universal Self.

— Sri Nityananda

I was in Delhi, India in 1984, when Prime Minister Indira Gandhi was assassinated by members of her own security guard. In the days that followed, I witnessed firsthand the horrors and brutality of inflamed passionate hatred and fear, of killing and maiming. At night, I would stand on the roof and count the fires burning throughout the city. I ventured outside during the day on a couple of occasions, despite the martial law forbidding this—the army patrols which roamed the city in trucks and jeeps had orders to shoot anyone. Once I saw a charred body sprawled in a park. I sat next to the corpse, and cried.

I am writing this chapter on March 16, 1998. A few of the magazines and newspapers close by mention the following events:

Today is the thirtieth anniversary of the incident in My Lai, where some 80 U.S. soldiers spent four hours killing 504 Vietnamese civilians, mostly women and children.

Within a three-month period in 1994, an estimated 800,000 people were killed in Rwanda, as a result of ethnic conflict between Hutus and Tutsis.

The Palestinian security chief warned Jewish settlers that they would "not leave alive" if they tried to attack residents of Hebron's Palestinian-ruled areas again.

The Bosnian-Serb army interned thousands of Moslem and Croatian women in camps where they were gang raped for weeks at a time to demoralize them.

Since the Chinese invaded Tibet in 1949, over one million people have been killed, and over 6,000 monasteries destroyed.

More than 25,000 people, most of whom will be civilians, will step on a land mine this year. According to the Red Cross, almost two million land mines are planted each year in killing fields around the world.

Metin Bakallci, who runs four Human Rights Foundation centers, said reports of torture in Turkey have declined in recent months because the police have developed methods that leave no traces—such as laying the victim on a block of ice before applying electric shocks.

A bomb exploded on a train in Punjab province, killing at least five people and injuring 20.

Is there a single place on this Earth where people are not committing or sponsoring violence, war, repression, and terror, militarily or economically, overtly or covertly? Is there a single place that has not been desecrated and ravaged, any single square inch of earth that has not been a burial ground? Is there any place where purity and innocence remain?

Let's be honest: the world is a spastic convulsion of violence, and we are that world. We must begin here; we must admit this truth without protest, embarrassment, or equivocation; without blame, defense, or explanation. It is true, pure and simple. Whatever peace exists is but a facade, behind which is more brutality. We must go beyond peace.

Peace, as the absence of conflict, violence, or war, may be achieved for a moment—but then that moment turns over and the dark side of peace breaks out, bombastic and vehement. This kind of peace is only a temporary suppression of violence. It may last a day, a year, or a hundred years; yet within this extended moment of peace the vibrating seeds of war are waiting to burst open. We must go beyond peace.

Wars do not end, because we have not found the courage to end violence within ourselves. We will stop only when we are willing to see the cause, only when we go beyond peace. Has peace ever been achieved, once and for all? No, it has not, because the peace we say we want, the peace we try and achieve, is not peace at all. It is only a suppression of violence.

Leaders must end violence within themselves, and end war in the world.

———————

The Sufi poet Rumi wrote, "A True Human Being is the essence, the original cause. The world and the universe are secondary effects." Our egos create these masks of secondary effects; our fear is our forgotten essence. If we are to find what is beyond peace, we must know who we are beyond our egos, our identities, our masks of secondary effects. We must know our essence, which loves without demand, lives without fear, serves without expectation.

Violence is the by-product of living within our defined identities: *man, woman; white, black; American, Israeli, Palestinian; Protestant, Catholic, Hindu, Sikh; Bloods, Crips; holy, sinful, pagan; heterosexual, homosexual.* Living within these identities, we are always afraid of the other, that which we are not. Our survival is dependent upon the survival of our identities, and those who are different will always be a threat. Even if peace and harmonious accord are established, fear remains. It is only a matter of time before we are again in conflict with the other. We will always be suspicious, and therefore afraid.

Peace is not a truce with violence, but a living return to the original cause, within which is an equilibrium that cannot be disturbed.

This equilibrium is waiting, just on the other side of nearby doors. One door is love. One door emanates beauty. One door opens a millisecond before death. Another door hangs poised between two thoughts, and another door rests like a harbor seal on the flat shiny rock of the breath as it pauses between in and out. There are many doors to that which is beyond peace.

Why then, if we want peace, do we not open these doors to our essence?

Leaders will live within the unbreakable silence of their essence. Leaders must go immediately through the doors to that which is beyond peace and war, beyond conflict and fear, beyond violence and ignorance. There is our home, there is our essence, there is our truth.

Leaders must go through these doors and never return. Leaders must know their essence. This is the way to end violence and hatred in the world. Leaders must have the courage to demonstrate this knowledge, and so to inspire it in others. Leaders must know how to meet another on the ground of original cause, original being, original essence. Leaders must meet others without fear, without desire, without identity.

Leaders must meet others in the spirit of that which is beyond peace.

How To
Change The World

Once you say "I want to find Truth," all your life will be deeply affected by it. All your mental and physical habits, feelings and emotions, desires and fears, plans and decisions will undergo a most radical transformation. To find truth, you must not cling to your convictions.

— NISARGADATTA MAHARAJ

I honor those who try to rid themselves of any lying, who empty the self and have only clear being there.

— RUMI

EVEN THOUGH THE TRUTH OF OUR BEING is present and revealed within us at all times, we do not usually experience this truth, know this truth, or speak this truth. We have to first work to get at it, and we have to work to live in it. After a while, living in the essential truth becomes natural, and we couldn't leave that truth even if we wanted to. It does take work and practice to find and experience and speak this truth of universal mystical essence. Until we do, we have to say that we are liars about life. This is not an accusation. However, if we do not tell the truth, then we tell lies. To tell the truth of who we are is difficult, though we must—all of us—now begin to do so. Certainly, leaders will have to do so, or they cannot be leaders.

Just as it is difficult to speak the inner truth, so is it difficult to speak the outer truth, to represent explicitly and precisely how we act and what we do—without anything else added. Just the bare presentation of facts, no extraneous adjectives or adverbs, only nouns and verbs: actions and items. *I threw this rock through that window.*

There is a strong correlation between being able to speak the truth of our inner being and being able to speak the truth of our outer actions. Both are essential. Both are hallmarks of leaders.

Telling the outer truth of our actions is difficult because, though we are told as children to tell the truth, most of us get into trouble when we tell the truth. "Did you take those cookies from the cookie jar?"

"Yes."

SMACK. We won't again admit that we took any cookies, not if it means getting hit on the head. We'll say, "No, I didn't. I swear I didn't. I think Rick did it."

We often make others uncomfortable when we speak the truth. We often elicit disapproval, or worse: *Do you have to say that? Why can't you be nice? Don't rock the boat. You're being disloyal. Let's just put that behind us. It's not nice to hurt someone's feelings. Don't rat on your friends. You should be ashamed of what you did.*

We quickly learn that telling the truth is risky business, so we learn how to obscure and spin the truth for approval, security, acceptance, to get what we want, to avoid punishment. We condition ourselves to instantly distort the true facts of our lives, so much so that we aren't able to know, within ourselves, what is true about our own motives, desires, and actions. The truth is terrifying to us.

In the late 1980's, I led a series of seminars in San Francisco, New York, and Boston. On the morning of the second day of a two-day seminar in Boston, we sat together in a truth circle. I asked everyone to consider saying something that they had never told anyone before, something they had kept secret and hidden from view.

The rationale for this exercise is simple: if we want to transform ourselves, to free ourselves from falsehood, to liberate ourselves from anxiety and fear and conditioning, to experience truth—then we will have to tell the truth. We will have to put our *actual* lives on the line. All transformation begins from where we are, by admitting what is true, what is actual, about our lives. This might be painful at first, but telling the truth will ultimately bring exquisite health, joy, and radiance to our lives: the truth will set us free.

The ground rule was that participation was voluntary. I was only offering the opportunity to explore the power of truth-telling.

In the first go around, people said things like *I stole a bag of candy when I was seven; I cheated on a math test; I blamed the broken vase on my brother; I lied on a job application.*

It was a beginning, albeit a modest one. I asked people how they felt when they spoke these previously unuttered truths. They felt relieved and somehow strengthened. I asked people how they felt about the others who had spoken these truths. They said they felt empathy. No one felt criticized, threatened, or judged.

I asked people to have another turn. I asked them to rummage through their boxes of forbidden experiences and bring one out. I reminded them to just say what happened and not add explanations or excuses; just say what happened. People reported truths that were a bit more revealing. The practice of the first round resulted in more significant tales. After this second round, we could feel a definite shift in awareness; we had come to a more acute state of attention. A new force, like a weather front, was gathering within each of us. A small truth had led to a larger truth; truth was catching hold. I asked people if they wanted to have a third try, and they said yes, they almost demanded it. They were ready, eager, anxious, to purge themselves of congestion and inhibitions and long-held fear and shame.

This time, people said things like *My father made me suck his penis every day for ten years, from the time I was five; One night last week I ate a large jar of peanut butter, two bags of Oreo cookies, and a one-pound bag of M&Ms and then made myself vomit—I've been doing things like that all my life; My father got so mad at me once that he killed my cat in front of me and nailed it to my bedroom wall; I masturbated with a crucifix; I stole about $25,000 worth of equipment from my employer and sold it in flea markets; I watched an elderly woman being beaten and robbed in a subway and did nothing to help her—I walked off the platform.*

Telling the truth requires practice. We have to learn how to get in touch with our inner and outer truths, and then we have to become fearless enough to speak those truths. This is the only way we will find out that truth has the power to liberate, to enliven, to empower—to free us from fear, shame, guilt. This is the only way that we can discover that we need not fear truth, that we can live and prosper in truth. Truth is a cleansing and purifying drink whose potency restores vitality, health, and radiance to our lives.

Telling the truth is hard and often terrifying. Sometimes we don't want to face what we actually do—we'd rather deny what we did, or find a way to pin the tail on someone else's donkey, because we may feel that the truth is too shameful. Alcohol and drug co-dependency, familial dysfunctions, sexual abuse, corporate and governmental fraud and corruption, police and military brutality—all of these exist as a function of secrecy, fear, intimidation, and shame. We often repress the truth of our actions and the actions of others through a personal code of denial, thinking this denial absolves us of responsibility and protects us from consequences.

Most of us also subscribe to another kind of self-protective code, a club code like the Mafia's code of *omerta,* silence. These codes are meant to protect people within a particular group from the inquiries of outsiders. Codes of self-protective silence prohibit truth and accountability, ensuring the group's survival. Almost every corporation, organization, institution, and bureaucracy—secular and religious—has a code of omerta every bit as perilous as the Mafia's.

People who break codes of silence and speak out on behalf of truth and accountability are often demonized, vilified, persecuted, imprisoned, even killed. These truth-tellers and boat-rockers are branded by others as heretics, pagans, traitors, whistle-blowers and are routinely condemned. Jeffrey Wigand is one such example. The vice president for research and development with Brown & Williamson Tobacco Corp. between 1989-93, he began to tell the truth about the tobacco industry. They, in turn, embarked on a campaign to discredit him, personally and professionally, and to sue him for violating the terms of his confidentiality agreement. It was made to seem that the larger crime was to reveal the truth, rather than what the truth revealed.

That's the way it usually works, although there appears to be a real outbreak of truth-telling and whistle-blowing going on in the world today. Whistle-blowers are very close to being saints. I would love to see a thousand saints of conscience wake up tomorrow and call a thousand press conferences.

Telling the truth is risky business, and it is tricky business too, because we each see the world differently. The various factors and conditions of our subjectivity—past experiences, self-image, race, national and religious affiliation, gender, language, mental acuity, emotional maturity, and so on— make it almost impossible to agree upon a consensus truth for anything. I am always interested in the feedback I receive after a seminar or talk. After one memorable evening of lively dialogue with a group, I was told that I was articulate, inspiring, powerful, arrogant, condescending, too mental, full of bullshit, witty, humorless, intense, and not intense enough.

It is also difficult to come to a common sense of truth because our thoughts and beliefs are self-justifying. Any strong thought or feeling we have about someone or something tends to define our truth. If someone hurts our feelings, or cheats us, or betrays a confidence, or does not return our love, we can quickly create a truth that is merely a function of our emotional reactivity.

Let me illustrate what I mean by telling the truth. In 1990, I moved from Mill Valley to Austin, Texas. I loaded up my rented U-Haul truck and drove away, following the route I plotted using a map from the local auto club. After two days of driving, I got to Austin. The map told the truth. If I had followed the map's route and ended up in Nashville, the map would have lied.

Can someone follow the directions of our words and get to the truth of what happened, or would they end up in New Orleans?

Leaders must be maps of unerring precision.

———————————

We have to start telling the truth, whether or not we want to be leaders. You and I must step forward and show the hand that threw the rock. The poet Robert Frost said that "anything more than the truth would be too much." We are in the

habit of saying much too much, spinning spun truths, hardly
ever speaking the actual truth.

On November 5, 1996, USA Today *reported the results of a
study conducted at RAND and the Harvard School of Public Health
that revealed the full extent of medical negligence in the U.S.
The annual toll of medical harm includes: 1.3 million injuries,
180,000 deaths, and total costs of $50 billion.*

There is a very practical reason for telling the truth.
Telling the truth makes what is real, real. A lie distorts the
simple fact of our actions and is composed, in varying
measure, of fantasy, denial, belief, rhetoric, dogma, fear,
guilt, shame, greed, anger, rationalization, and justification.
Relative to actual events, a lie is unreal, and the truth is real,
and nothing is more practical than reality.

When we speak lies, we create an unreal world, an
abstract world. If our lies have force and conviction, which
they usually do, we end up believing them ourselves. We then
live in this unreal, abstract world. We grow up in this world.
We go to school in this world. We work in this world. We try
to solve problems in this world. We marry and have children
in this world. We pray and worship in this world. We grow
old and die in this world. The celluloid world of movies is
more real than this unreal world of our lies.

It is hard to tell the truth; still, we must enter the actual
world of how we are and of what we do. If we don't, how
will we ever be able to change what needs to be changed,

to fix what is broken, to soothe what hurts, to find love in a joyous world? We must start telling the truth, the whole truth—not just the distorted truth, the partial truth, the half truth, the truth that makes us look good by deflecting culpability, or sells our product, or wins that contract, or gets us elected. The whole truth. Anything less is a lie.

When we tell the truth, the picture and the possibilities change. When we tell the truth, the real world appears. When the real world appears, it is not as terrifying as we imagined it would be. We can begin to work with what is, in the real world. As painful as the truth circles were, everyone felt a tremendous relief after telling truths, after admitting to themselves and to others that something was so. It really is no big deal. What is a big deal, what is a terrible deal, is the false, unreal, abstract world of lies. It is like living in hell. It is hell. It is the weirdest failure of all.

For the sixth year in a row, the U.S. maintained its lead as the world's major exporter of bombs, tanks, and jet fighters.

Telling the truth is synonymous with leadership. To tell the truth, one must know the truth, and to know the truth, one must seek the truth. Seeking, knowing, and telling the simple truth is the sum total of a leader's work.

Leadership's single principle, single value, single tenet, single model, single paradigm, single strategy, goal, and objective is to tell the truth. If we don't do this, this world,

which was made as a paradise, will become an unendurable
hell.

Tell the truth.

Tell the truth.

Tell the truth.

We have to get very serious about this, very unforgiving of
leadership liars. We must absolutely expect and demand the
truth. We cannot turn away from this. We've got to plug in
our bullshit meters, and when the needle hits red, we have
to speak up. Loudly. Persistently. We must learn to live in
the real world.

We must categorically demand truth and accountability
from our leaders, and we cannot allow them to hide behind
any shields.

The ashram's basic law was *Show up or be gone,* and leadership's basic law is *Tell the truth or be gone.*

To become more aware, more conscious, more friendly
with reality requires that we make the covert, overt; it
requires that we reveal secrets; it requires truth and accountability. Every person in every corporation, organization,
institution, or bureaucracy—secular and religious—could
help the cause of reality by telling the truth.

Once we invite reality into our house, we can move the
chairs around if we need to, cook more food, do whatever
we need to make reality a comfortable and happy guest in
our home. But first things first: we must tell the truth.
Indulge this fantasy:

Yes, my company manufactures, markets, and sells cigarettes. This
product kills a half a million people in America each year—and
two and a half million more per year around the world—inflicts
untold suffering on millions of others, and costs America as much as
$100 billion dollars a year. In the past, this company has tried to
boost nicotine's potency to more easily addict smokers, this company
has studied ways to attract the attention of children so that they
would want to buy our product. This company has woven a 40-year
old tapestry of lies, deceit, corruption, and greed. Ranking members
of this company have lied under oath to Congress, the American
people, and the world.

The truth is a powerful force. Telling the truth is the first
step, accountability—ownership of actions—is the second.
Accountability opens the way for penance, healing, forgive-
ness, change, and transformation. Telling the truth
automatically reveals accountability. The fantasy continues:

In telling the truth, I have to admit that it was me, not a
company, who has been making and selling this deadly product.
In telling the truth, I am able to see the consequences of my own
actions. I cannot hide any longer. I can no longer hide what I know;
I can no longer argue that people should be free to buy what they
want to buy. The simple truth is that I should not make such a
product, which is far deadlier than crack cocaine and heroin. If I
continue, I am a brother of the Colombian drug lords. Are my fields
of tobacco less a killing field than the world's cocoa plant and opium
poppy fields? Having told the truth, I can see all of this now, and it
is terrible. I don't know what I was thinking. As of this moment,
I will stop. I will find another way to make a living and support

my family. Now that I have told the truth, now that I have seen the reality of what I have done, I cannot do this any longer.

Telling the truth means we know what we are doing. Being accountable means that we know who's doing it. When we know what we are doing and who's doing it, we can then change and transform, not before. Truth, accountability, transformation: this is the holy trinity which will save us from ourselves.

This world is our world. Whatever exists in our world exists because we have created it. Once we accept this, we can change what we want to change. We have the power to re-create our creation. But we have to tell the truth and be accountable.

In a recent television discussion between the Reverend Jerry Falwell and Mr. Larry Flynt, publisher of *Hustler Magazine,* Mr. Flynt said, "I am a businessman. My magazine is a reflection of what people want. It does not represent what I want. I just give people what they want."

I don't object to Mr. Flynt's comment on ethical, moral, or aesthetic grounds. I do, however, object to his statement on the grounds of accountability, or rather the lack of it. "Giving people what they want" is a marketing commandment. It is also the very summit of unaccountability.

"I'm just doing my job" is another summit in the mountain range of this foolishness. "I was just doing my job" could be called the Nuremberg defense. It is ludicrous. Leaders will never say "I'm just giving people what they want" or "I'm just doing my job," because they have too much respect for truth and accountability.

Leaders understand that if we can first bring the actual world forward, we can then bring the real world forward. Leaders who find the courage to stand up in the truth, to be accountable in the truth, will change what must be changed.

Let's become a nation of whistle-blowing, boat-rocking renegades soaked in truth-telling and drenched in account-ability. Let us do so for love of freedom and truth and reality, with respect and love and compassion. This is a voluntary exercise. It is not another excuse for witch-hunts and burn-ings. This is not an opportunity to cast out another's demons for the sake of our own fear or anger or guilt or shame. We tell the truth here, inside ourselves, in our own home. We say, *Yes, I threw this rock through that window;* or we say, *No, I did not throw this rock through that window.* Both statements must be a map that will get us to Austin.

Let's bring the actual world forward, and then the real world. Let's bring our actual selves forward, and then our real selves. Let us find out whether or not the truth will set us free and, if it does, then let's learn how to live freely, in joy, in love, and in truth. Leaders will live in truth and accountability, setting themselves free and inspiring us to experience that same freedom.

The Creative Power

Now let's talk about that nasty stuff that everyone likes to hear about, you know—SEX. This is the point from which we are all jet-propelled. With it you can reach the stars, or beat yourself to pieces against the rocks. Or, if you are very fortunate, enjoy unendurable pleasure, indefinitely prolonged.

    — JOE MILLER

It is in this union between the masculine and the feminine, which is a creative and erotic act, that all the forms of the universe are born.

    — MARGOT ANAND

Indeed, patriarchal religions throughout the ages had people killed off for being sexually alive. The human body and its erotic power became a source of evil. What if, instead, it would have been considered a source of divine embodiment?

    — MARYSE CÔTÉ

ON THE FIRST DAY OF ANY CLIENT'S INDIVIDUAL RETREAT, I schedule them for an extended session of bodywork with a masseuse. Massage is wonderful; its effect relaxes the body, stills the mind, and liberates the spirit. It is the perfect entree to meditation, and meditation is the perfect entree to awareness and contact with reality.

One particular client told me he had never been massaged, had never experienced bodywork. With some trepidation, he agreed to it. I brought in my top gun, an associate who was not only an extraordinary masseuse, but also a highly skilled intuitive. I had come to value her insights about other clients, which she discerned from their physical bodies as well as their subtle energy bodies. She would often see images, symbolic of the client's beliefs or of repressed prior events, which proved to be accurate and useful.

She came upstairs to my office after her first session with this client, collapsed into a chair, and sighed. She was exhausted.

What happened to you? I asked.

I'm going to raise my rates she joked. *I've never, ever, not in the hundreds of people I've worked with, ever experienced anyone so closed. He is not made of flesh, but of concrete. There is no life force moving in him; his body is almost dead. All his energy is in his head. He can only think. He can't feel his emotions or his body. I kept getting images of fear and shame: I think he's terrified of his body, embarrassed by it, and has closed off to physical pleasure. He's totally guilty about sex. Does he get angry a lot?*

Yes. People never know when he's going to go off.

Too bad he doesn't get off. His anger is really his fear of himself, of his own body.

Does it seem inappropriate to speak about sex in a book that purports to be about leadership? It isn't, especially in this book. Leadership is an accord with reality, with the cosmos, with the primal life force, with that rapture of being which exists beyond the fear-based atmosphere of ego identities.

The mystical experience is, in a manner of speaking, orgasmic: it is deeply blissful, peaceful, energizing, unifying, ecstatic. The mystical life is a deepening of intimacy and friendship with reality; mystics become the love-force within the life force. Mystics become sensitized to subtleties of perception, sensation, and feeling; their bodies are not transcended but transmuted: from concrete to stamen, from fear to love, from shame to joy.

The new species of leader is a mutant creature, the illicit offspring of a savagely beautiful midnight coupling.

Back in their heyday, the Monty Python comedy troupe wrote a skit in which one of the characters responded to the question "What are your hobbies?" with, "Strangling animals, golf, and masturbation." The BBC censors would not permit the word masturbation on British television. The skit was aired, but with the offensive word deleted.

It was, apparently, inoffensive to strangle animals, but offensive to touch one's own body in a pleasurable manner. We in America are every bit as uptight and fearful of sex as the British censors. There is tremendous ambivalence towards sexuality in our culture, and it is certainly something

for leaders to become aware of and resolve within themselves.

We are entranced by sex and sexual imagery, by eroticism,
and at the same time we condemn and vilify our own delight
and interest. On the one hand, sexual imagery is the mainstay
of corporate advertising; sex and nudity are sure ways to
guarantee box office receipts and are the cornerstone of most
TV tabloid and talk shows; revelations of the sexual orienta-
tion of celebrities will make the magazines fly off the stands,
and stories of politicians' sexual shenanigans can ruin careers.
Adult services, books, magazines, videos, and merchandise
are a multi-billion dollar industry. On the other hand, we
prohibit ourselves from speaking openly about sex, our
children from learning about it, our teachers from teaching
it. Is it any wonder that it took Ronald Reagan years to even
say the word AIDS?

We would sooner speak of strangling animals than sex.

Sexual energy is creative energy; it is the energy of life
itself—the ecstatic creative impulse of primordial consciousness. As we try to regulate and repress it through fear, shame,
and guilt we become estranged from that very force which
created us, and the world, and the universe. We become
afraid of intimacy with the very cause of our existence. This
is a supremely weird failure of self-betrayal.

We should not be afraid of sex, or the organs of sex,
because penises and vaginas are everywhere: every living
thing is born of sex. Sex is everywhere, as strong and heady

and dizzying as crushed gardenias. Each cell of each living thing is sexual, in its own way. Even stars are born through the stupendous sexual encounters of forces, male and female, copulating to the music of God.

When we repress our life force, it can only be expressed in twisted and angry and shameful ways. If we allow what is natural to come out from its underground hiding places, we will see that we do not need to be afraid of sex, of sexuality, of eroticism, of pleasure, of bodily ecstasy and intimacy and love.

We secretly long for our bodies to sing, but publicly we get angry at sex and at sexual people and sexual things. We forbid intimacy with certain parts of the body, though we dream of it.

Really, the problem is not with sex, the problem is with our guilt and shame about sex, and our fear of surrendering to the creative pulse and vibration of reality. Fear, shame, and guilt—not sex—are our problems. These create the distorting torque of natural sexual expression.

If we cannot love this creative source of life, we cannot love life. If we repress the sexual energy, we suppress life, creativity, joy, and love. If we control and regulate our bodies because we are afraid of joy and pleasure, we will become angry and our anger will lash out at others, whose bodies are also our body, at animals, whose bodies are also our body, at the world, whose body is also our body.

If we cannot love the sacred pleasures and transcendent beauty of our own body, if we cannot sink our separate body into another's and thus find the single body of our true being, if we cannot fearlessly love and be loved, pleasure and be pleasured, then how will we ever love reality? How will we ever delight in this world? How will we ever know communion with another?

Leaders will not be afraid of sex. They will love the very creative power which created them. They will worship this energy, dissolve in this energy, and flood the world with this energy.

An interesting sub-culture is emerging in America: sexual healers. These are women and men who have studied the ancient sexual/spiritual path toward mystical union with reality. Leaders might want to study in the dojos of these healers and teachers of sacred sexuality. They can show us how to release our fear and guilt and shame of our bodies, how to befriend sexual energy, how to blend with the creative power. We must learn to delight in the eroticism of life. We must become skillful and articulate about sex, eroticism, pleasure. We must speak openly of these things.

Many people in our society have renounced the unquenchably ecstatic nature of physical reality in the name of one belief or another, or of fear, shame, or guilt. Leaders will need to announce, not renounce, the ecstatic nature of physical living.

Leaders should visit the temples of sexual healing and learn from their priestesses and priests. Leaders will consecrate their own bodies to joyous and ecstatic living. Leaders must learn to touch everything with the hand of a lover seeking only to give pleasure and love. Through sacred loving the soul becomes the body, the spirit becomes the flesh, the world becomes heaven.

Eating Eternity

Everything depends on this: a fathomless sinking into a fathomless nothingness.

— JOHANNES TAULER

To turn that magnificence out there into reasonableness doesn't do anything for you. Here, surrounding us, is eternity itself. To engage in reducing it to a manageable nonsense is petty and outright disastrous.

— DON JUAN MATUS

I WOULD NOT TRUST ANYONE TO LEAD who does not know eternity, and who cannot speak about it in a compelling way. Leaders are the offshoots of eternity and they must know this as an experienced fact. The leader's power derives from eternity, and the leader's skill and cunning from ageless wisdom. The leadership agenda is knowing this reality and serving the life behind all life.

On a warm summer day in Santa Barbara, I had lunch with eternity.

I was a participant with about 20 others in a meeting
whose purpose was to inquire into truth. The meeting was
led by Jean Klein, an elderly Belgian teacher of non-dualism.
We were sitting in folding chairs or cross-legged on the car-
peted floor or on the couch that had been moved to the back
of the large living room. Jean was perhaps 80 at the time,
white haired and translucent, the embodiment of silence. He
was like a waterfall of pure acceptance, and standing beneath
his spray I breathed with lungs I didn't know I had.

He would say a few words, and then silence. Someone
might venture a question. He would respond, and then more
silence. We passed the morning like that. His speaking was
itself a form of silence, each word coming slowly, with precision, from a deep well. You could almost hear his mind falling
like an empty pail into an invisible depth, filling, and then
being drawn up by his careful voice.

We stopped at about noon, and went outside for lunch. I
sat with Jean and a few others at a picnic table. We ate slowly,
silently, still appreciating the atmosphere of the morning. It
seemed to me that we were all attentive, mindful of what
we were saying and doing, respectful of others, listening with
our entire bodies to the total environment. It was natural,
without technique or effort. It was simply a condition that
had been established of its own accord. If someone or something moved, everything moved in unison. Perfect timing,
perfect relationship, perfect understanding.

We ate ice cream for dessert. Then, as we sat together on
the benches with elbows and forearms collapsed on the table-
top, the world dissolved.

I took a breath, and it was my last. *There is perception, but no perceiver! There is perception, but no perceived! All worry is worry about me and my body; I'm just an idea and it's not really worth worrying about. Love is this...no other...nothing other...only this wholeness...*

Everything I've ever thought is just ridiculous. My God, we should all just sit down and shut up and not move—that would really be the best thing. What are these electrical flashes and currents? This is all energy! Pure energy, vibrating and singing!

I simply disappeared, but remained present, as an awareness. I looked up and saw the sky and the clouds, but the seeing was with eyes that were not mine. I looked at the others, and saw myself. Everything was bright and radiant. It was so simple and so awesome. There were cognitions, but they were too fine for words, and they passed quickly, as a silent commentary on the pure feeling of just being, everywhere at once.

It seemed that everything was alive in a way I had never noticed. The grass of the lawn, the dirt clumps at the base of a lemon tree, its bark; at the end of the bench was a woman whose hair shone; the air itself—all this was alive, breathing, growing, moving in *something,* a kind of force, a comforting presence. When I looked at something, it looked back. There was no separation, no difference. I did not own this seeing; it was not mine, not my eyes.

A cognition that came several times was *how beautiful, how beautiful.* I thought of all I had read and studied and learned, all I had experienced: laughter. I thought of all my worries and fears and hopes: laughter. I thought of myself: laughter. It was pure laughter, joyous as never before, not because of anything, but in and of itself. Who was thinking, I don't know. Who was laughing, I don't know. There was no solid center, no place I could call me. Like salt in water, I lost my granular self, but lived as everyone, as everything.

It was the most marvelous calamity, the most terrific loss: a falling away of self, all in an instant. I knew, without knowing, this creation is alive and conscious. This creation is beautiful, this creation is beheld silently in wonder and awe. A conscious presence lives at the center of all things, underneath all things, within all things. There is an order to life that is out of time. It is eternal, but fully present and revealed in each moment, in each thing. The silence grew deeper and the loss more total.

There was just pure existence. If there was thought or movement, if there was discussion and laughter, it happened by itself, to no one in particular. Things seemed far off because they happened to no one, but everything glowed brightly, clearly, so full of *itself,* the presence.

So much was lost, and so much gained. It was so apparent, how did I miss it? Here, now, in this very minute, as we are, seated at a picnic table, eating ice cream, is depth upon depth of loveliness and silent beauty. *My God, how much I love this creation that I am!*

There is so much order, intelligence, and fullness in the creation that we are. There is so much beauty, so much love, so much tenderness. This is what reality is. We find ourselves in this loss of self, in the opening to mystery, in seeing the conscious presence that brightens all things.

I would say that we must realize this, but it is already realized. I would say that we must return to this seeing and knowing, but we have never left. I would say that we must find this within ourselves, but it is not lost. I can only affirm that we are this silent beauty, that we do live as the living presence in all things, that we are love.

I want to hear leaders speak of this. I want decisions to be made in the light of this reality. I want the silence of eternity to be the foremost advisor of leaders everywhere.

If leaders will serve eternity, the world will sleep well.

TWENTY-ONE

A Spectacle of Silence

*Whenever the internal dialogue stops, the world collapses and
extraordinary facets of ourselves surface, as though they had been
heavily guarded by our words. You are like you are, because you
tell yourself that you are that way.*

    — DON JUAN MATUS

Knock on the sky and listen to the sound!

    — ZEN SAYING

I WITNESSED A SPECTACLE OF SILENCE in the Berkeley
Community Theater, located at 1930 Alston Way, Berkeley,
California. Every one of the 3,491 seats was occupied. On
stage sat Thich Nhat Hanh, a Vietnamese Buddhist monk.
Next to him sat a young woman. The monk spoke about
mindfulness, about awareness, about respect for each other
and all living things. He spoke slowly and quietly. From time
to time he would fall silent, and the woman would pick up
and ring a bell that rested on the floor in front of her. The
reverberations of the bell could be heard throughout the

auditorium and felt within each person's brain, stimulating perceptions of intuitive subtlety.

Thich Nhat Hanh's talk was less about information than experience. The words were like a tour bus carrying the audience past ancient sites of meaning and depth and beauty. Though the bus was still and unmoving, we traveled far and saw much. Anyone could have dropped a tack or a nail file, even a piece of paper, and the noise would have seemed loud because the silence was so great.

After some time, I felt the audience breathe in unison, a meditative breathing, a breathing that connected us together and to the awareness of which the monk was speaking. I thought I was sitting in the mountains at twilight, when life itself begins to creep from its hiding places like a deer come to drink from a lake of pentagrams and stars.

Even when speaking, the monk was silent, was silence. To hear, the audience had to be silent and become silence. It was a spectacle. We were embraced by silence and thus set free from agitation, from separation, from duality. It would have been impossible for any anger or cruelty to arise in that community. It would have been impossible for anyone to harm another in any way. We were transported to reality.

The world needs this silence. Leaders, like the monk, will be of this silence. Their minds will be silent, their actions will be silent, their hearts will be silent.

Silence cannot be explained. It is not knowable, nor can it be experienced in a way that might be familiar to us, as we are used to experiencing other events in our life.

We can only use words to point in the direction of silence, such that if one actually goes into the distance towards which the words point, one will eventually come upon silence as a fact. When silence is beheld as a fact, all speculation, argument, and belief about that to which the word silence refers ends instantly and forever.

Silence is that in which everything exists, from which everything comes, and into which everything returns. It is the unutterable context in which the cosmos occurs, a playground of pure consciousness.

Silence is oneness. Silence refers to a state of fundamental unified existence, a condition of being in which all conflict, fear, doubt, projection, memory, delusions—all subjectivity and objectivity—are dissolved and thus resolved. Silence is an instantaneous recognition of that which is out of time and unconditioned by cause and effect. If one were a religious person, one could say that silence is the soul of God, or perhaps the God of God.

If this sounds abstract, vague, or esoteric, it only sounds so because we cannot say exactly what silence is. Some things are so very beyond the reach of words and metaphors, symbols and images, beliefs and concepts that all attempts to describe them are foolish. And yet, even as we speak foolishly and impertinently of that which cannot be said, something within us will smile knowingly. It is this intuitive resonance which words can stimulate. This is the direction we can point to and go toward, walking or running, in order for the recognition of the wordless to become real. But even as silence becomes indomitably real, as taut and tense and thrilling as a tidal wave crashing upon us, crushing us beyond recognition—even as this happens, we cannot speak its truth.

Any disciplined practice that involves focusing the mind will eventually lead to silence. Spiritual methods such as meditation techniques, chanting mantras, yoga, tai chi—all of these will lead to silence. Self-inquiry will lead to silence. So will martial arts, and dance, and art. So will rock climbing and sky-diving. So will cooking and eating. So will playing and loving. Everything will lead to silence, because silence is the life force behind everything. It is the oxygen without which everything would fall over dead, flash frozen.

Being led to silence might imply that silence is somewhere else. This is only a figure of speech. Silence is always the first thing and the last thing. It is always present, but very subtle, so we must therefore learn to recognize it. The direction of silence is any direction. There is no place that silence is not, although we cannot apprehend it with our senses or with our minds.

Still, let me suggest a fool-proof way of coming into silence quickly, so that silence becomes a fact for us. First, we must develop the ability to distinguish one thought from another. When we can do this, we must then develop the ability to see clearly the space between two thoughts. When that space becomes large and stable enough for us to drive a truck through it, we will know silence as a fact.

The underlying truth of existence is silence. States of mind, states of being, are definable and contained within time and space. Silence is not definable. Silence is not a state because a state refers to something that one can achieve or

enter, and if one can achieve or enter it, one can then lose it
or leave it.

In the very center of universal manifestation, one finds
swirling gusts of silence, vast galactic streamers millions of
light years long. If we try to understand this silence through
our mind, we'll never understand it. Silence is realized in a
moment of communion, in a moment of losing our separation from life.

Silence embraces everything and cannot be known because
to know silence, we would have to be separate from silence,
and silence would then be an object of our perception and
of our knowing. Silence refers to that which is beyond this
dualism of knower and known. We might say that silence is
love, or beauty, or grace. Silence becomes a fact when we and
life become an inseparable whole. Even though we are trying
to define it, no definition of silence is accurate. We don't
want to think that by defining it, we can know it. Silence is
knowable only to itself, and we come into that knowing
through an alchemy of self-transcendence.

We can only create a definition that points to silence. The
truth of reality is silent. It is undisturbed. It is causeless. It is
out of time, out of space, non-dual. Silence is the preeminent
nothingness in which the universe dances in spectacular and
mysterious ways.

If silence is the United States, then intuition is Ellis Island,
the first stop of immigrants seeking asylum. Intuition is the
first hint, the first experience of the far greater country of
silence. Intuition is not a tool, but rather an intelligence that

uses us. We might not see this right away. Intuition is willing to be used, but only for a time. One day, it will require that we suspend our goals and objectives, our plans and aspirations, for a fuller recognition of what intuition is, what it represents. We will come to see that intuition is the ambassador of silence, and we must serve that silence, for it is the soul of the world.

In the instant of intuitive perception, we are taken wholly into that power of knowing which is beyond the mind. In going beyond the mind, we go beyond all notions of self and identity, of thought and belief, of perceiver and perceived. A photograph of the intuitive flash would show only light. There would be no other image, only light. The light of intuition is the light of consciousness. Intuition is Ellis Island, the gateway to freedom. In order to be free, we must want freedom, we must be willing to leave behind the old countries of control and manipulation from which we have come. We cannot come to this new country with ideas of exploitation, as gangsters. We have to come as servants of the new freedom. We have to learn new ways of living. We have to become students of silence and freedom in order to learn how to live without fear, without violence, without cruelty.

Leaders are students and servants of silence.

Silence is practical. Intuition is practical. Both will show us how to live now, in the present, attending to the needs of the moment.

A few years ago, in conversation with the president of a manufacturing company, I heard about "just-in-time manufacturing," also referred to as "continuous flow." The idea is to produce goods to coincide with orders: no inventory, no warehousing: nothing is produced before its appointed time.

It occurred to me that there is also a "just-in-time knowing" where one learns to trust that one will know what one needs to know when one needs to know it. We don't have to stockpile plans, beliefs, and fantasies about the future. We can meet life with an empty personal warehouse, and when a demand is made, the revelation will be produced.

This attitude implies that one does not need to have it all figured out ahead of time, but that one can quench one's thirst for knowing by dropping an empty pail into the unfathomable well of *now*.

Leadership is strengthened by the leader's respectful relationship to "not knowing." While most people press and strain to know everything in a definitive way, the leader would be better served to be at peace with simultaneously knowing and not knowing. Siddhartha learned to wait while listening to the flowing river, ultimately learning the secrets of the universe. So, too, the head of a company must have a great capacity to wait for the right moment in which to know and act; to wait for the auspicious alignment of forces or people or circumstances.

This waiting can be frustrating to others who are not similarly disposed. It can also appear to be uncertainty, vagueness, even weakness. A leader is often pressured by others to be definitive about both the present and the future. People want their leaders to provide irrefutable direction, to resolve the ambiguities of living and working that seem to crowd in on us more and more. I often hear people screaming silently, "Just tell me what, where, when and how!" both in business and in life. Answers to those questions are like the weather in the Swiss Alps: ferociously unpredictable and changeable.

Conventional business ideology urges us to develop a strategic plan of the future, a blueprint for success which everyone will believe in and rally around. But creative planning is primarily derived from observing the intricacies of *now*. It is a skill that requires depth in listening, patience in action, and harmonious relationship with all things, not just one's strategic plan. It requires one to master the insistent pressures of one's own mind and to learn how to thrive and prosper within the basic uncertainty of living.

Just-in-time knowing does not handicap us; in fact, it links us to a clarity that cannot be known otherwise. This clarity is the reflection of what is actually occurring; it is a combination of subtle perception, insight, and intuition. Our capacity to act with this clarity is what generates the most appropriate response in every situation, because this clarity is a function of relating to and assimilating the late breaking news of a continuously flowing reality. People plan because they can't see what is happening. People control because they are not in accord with the organic and evolutionary continuous flow of nature, of silence.

The inspiration, vision, and purpose which originates from this clarity is *seen* within the very fabric of the unfolding present, not fabricated or created by disparate strands of desire and hope and ambition. This clarity of knowing wells up within us from the central intelligence agency of life itself.

Our future is most assured if our present is in accord with this intelligence.

Wise leaders discover what to do, when and how, by continuously relating to and flowing with everything that is happening, which in turn deepens their connection to the living present. By honoring the living present, they receive its treasure of wisdom that cannot be known ahead of time, but just in time. Visions, goals, and plans all come about spontaneously in silence when a leader expresses the basic intention to live in accord with the intelligent force of life itself.

We have to let go of the bar. We will not fall. We will be held by silence. We don't need to know, but to be. This is not weakness, it is strength. Rumi wrote, "Do you think I know what I'm doing? That for one breath or half-breath I belong to myself? As much as a pen knows what it's writing, or the ball can guess where it's going next."

Silence knows what must be written, and silence knows where the ball is going to go next. We must only know silence. The world needs this silence. The world needs leaders who know and serve silence.

Whirling Dervishes

Here's the new rule: Break the wineglass, and fall towards the Glassblower's breath.

    — R U M I

I don't want to be the only one here telling all the secrets—filling up all the bowls at this party, taking all the laughs. I would like you to start putting things on the table that can also feed the soul the way I do. That way we can invite a hell of a lot more friends.

    — H A F I Z

To ASK LEADERS TO KNOW REALITY is to ask them to cross a crucible of glowing coals with bare feet. At first look, it seems impossible: the beds of red- and white-hot coals cannot be walked on without incinerating the feet. Reality is too far away, to impossible to know.

In 1994, I was asked by a client to design a three-day retreat for his company. We established the themes as leadership, customer service, teamwork, and unprecedented levels of performance. This last one was our real focus: how to teach and inspire people to do things they've never done before. The retreat was named "Climbing the Mountain," and was held at Snowbird, Utah during the summer.

On the second evening we went outside, all 220 of us, and gathered in a large field surrounded by craggy mountain ridges painted with the fading colors of dusk.

We built three pyres of wood, set each on fire, and waited for the structures to collapse in heaps of coals and embers. They knew what was coming; we had spoken about walking across the beds of coals inside.

The group was diverse: men and women from 19 to 84, all sizes, shapes, and colors, many different nationalities and religions. Almost to a one, they thought they wouldn't be able to walk across the coals.

As we waited, drummers drummed and dancers whirled around the fires.

When the pyres collapsed we separated into three smaller groups, with the people of each one taking turns raking the coals into 14 foot rectangles. By now it was dark, and the sparks from the glowing beds lifted up into the night like crazy fireflies.

Drummers pounded on the big drumheads, slowly and rhythmically. People stood silently in their groups, waiting to do, to be, the impossible. Who would go first? Would anyone?

Someone yelped, broke from the crowd, and ran across. Cheers and screams rose with the sparks and brightened the sky.

The drummers quickened the beat.

Another cry, another runner. Then another. The drumming boomed.

Two hundred twenty faces shone red in the night. Two hundred twenty people caught the fire of freedom. Another runner, then another, too many to watch at once, too many to count.

One by one, then in twos and sometimes threes—holding hands, cheering, singing, shouting, crying—people ran across, then danced across. Everyone went once, most twice, some wouldn't stop. The drummers' mallets pounded on the drumheads, throwing huge sounds up and against the cliffs. The runners and dancers lived on the coals, walked across, stood for minutes.

Everyone danced and whirled across the crucible of impossibility.

In the 13th century, the Persian mystic Jelaluddin Rumi founded a sect of Sufism known as the whirling dervishes. Rumi said, "Let us whirl like a compass around the point of divine grace." One does not need to be a Sufi to be a whirling dervish. The dervish's dance is a universal dance, the dervish's turning is the celebration of life, the dervish's whirl is the elaborate soul of the cosmos.

I have seen Sufis dance in this way, arms outstretched, heads erect, turning and turning, twirling and whirling faster and faster, always precise and perfect, until they abandon their forms for formlessness, until their physical bodies become spiritual bodies, until they leave the visible world and enter the invisible, still dancing, turning and turning, lost and found in love-making of exquisite subtlety, sinking into unfathomable depths of rapture and rising to majestic heights of self-release, spinning and turning, turning and dancing, succumbing again and again to the precious delightful essence in which all life turns and dances in freedom, in joy, in love— and then, after hours, maybe days, maybe weeks, the turning and turning slowly slows, the rapture of formlessness becomes the ecstasy of form, the invisible world becomes the visible, the inner becomes the outer: the world becomes the point of divine grace.

The whirling dervish is a gift of the invisible world to the visible world. Our world needs leaders who know how to whirl, who do whirl, who will teach us how to whirl.

Our world needs invisible leaders who are seen only as beauty where beauty is, as kindness where kindness is, as joy where joy is, as truth where truth is, as awareness where awareness is, as life where life is.

Our world needs invisible leaders who speak from the tiniest house of time, whose intoxicating fragrance reminds us of our own, who have visited eternity, who know what death knows.

Our world needs leaders who live in silence and speak silently. Our world needs leaders who serve our mystic soul, the same one that we all share, the same one that we each are.

Our world needs leaders whose eyes we trust, whose heart we know, whose soul is rampant in all that they do, seen and unseen, heard and unheard, done and not done.

Our world was made to whirl like a compass around the point of divine grace. Our world needs leaders whose only turning is this turning.

Will you be one?

Selected Bibliography

Barks, Coleman (tr.), *The Hand of Poetry: Five Mystic Poets of Persia*, Omega Publications, New Lebanon, NY, 1993.

———, *Feeling the Shoulder of the Lion*, Threshold Books, Putney, VT, 1991.

———, *This Longing: Poetry, Teaching Stories, and Letters of Rumi*, Threshold Books, Putney, VT, 1988.

Bly, Robert (tr.), *The Kabir Book*, The Seventies Press, 1977.

Bridle, Susan, "An Interview with Margo Anand," *What is Enlightenment?*, Issue 13, Spring/Summer 1998.

Brunner, Borgna (ed.), *1998 Information Please Almanac*, Information Please LLC, Boston, 1997.

Castaneda, Carlos, *The Teachings of Don Juan: A Yaqui Way of Knowledge*, University of California Press, Berkeley, CA, 1986.

Chollet, Laurence B., "Seven Years in Tibet," *Shambhala Sun*, September 1997.

Earth Island Journal, San Francisco, Volume 13, Number 1, Winter 1997-98.

Forsyth, Karl, "Television Robs Our Children of Their Potential," Computers in Education web site (http://www.corecom.net/~karlfpp/asd-comp.htm).

Hanh, Thich Nhat, *Being Peace,* Parallax Press, Berkeley, CA, 1987.

Hatengdi, M. U., and Swami Chetanananda, *Nitya Sutras: The Revelations of Nityananda from the Chidakash Gita,* Rudra Press, Cambridge, MA, 1985.

Havel, Václav, "The Need for Transcendence in the Postmodern World," Independence Hall, Philadelphia, PA, 1994, Václav Havel web site (http://www.hrad.cz/president/Havel /speeches/index_uk.html).

Jensen, Carl, *20 Years of Censored News,* Seven Stories Press, New York, 1997.

Krishnamurti, J. K., *Freedom From The Known,* Harper & Row, New York, 1969.

———, *You Are The World,* Harper & Row, New York, 1972.

Klein, Jean, *I Am,* Third Millennium Publications, Santa Barbara, CA, 1989.

———, *The Ease of Being,* The Acorn Press, Durham, NC, 1984.

Ladinsky, Daniel (tr.), *The Subject Tonight is Love: 60 Wild and Sweet Poems of Hafiz,* Pumpkin House Press, North Myrtle Beach, SC, 1996.

Macy, Joanna, "The Great Turning," *Connections Magazine,* Sausalito, CA, Issue 3, February 1998.

Mitchell, Jennifer D., "Editorial: The Tigers," *World•Watch,* Washington, D.C., Vol. 11, No. 1, January/February 1998.

Moyne, John, and Coleman Barks (tr.), *Unseen Rain: Quatrains of Rumi,* Threshold Books, Putney, VT, 1986.

————, *Say I am You,* Maypop, Athens, GA, 1994. Nisargadatta, Sri Maharaj, I Am That, The Acorn Press, Durham, NC, 1982.

Paine, Thomas, *Common Sense,* 1776.

Pearce, Joseph Chilton, *Evolution's End: Claiming the Potential of Our Intelligence,* Harper Collins, New York, 1992.

Pine, Red (tr.), *The Zen Teaching of Bodhidharma,* North Point Press, San Francisco, 1989.

Power, Richard (ed.), *Great Song: The Life and Teachings of Joe Miller,* Maypop, Athens, GA, 1993.

Renesch, John (pub.), *The New Leaders,* Sterling & Stone, San Francisco, Spring 1994.

Robbins, John, *Diet for a New America,* Stillpoint Publishing, Walpole, NH, 1987.

Robbins, Tom, "The Meaning of Life," Special Supplement Insert, *Life Magazine,* Vol. 14, No. 16, December 1991.

Russell, Peter, *The Brain Book,* E. P. Dutton, Inc., New York, 1979, pp. 212-213

Schiller, David, *The Little Zen Companion,* Workman Publishing, New York, 1994.

Smithsonian World: The Quantum Universe, Unapix, New York, 1996.

Thoreau, Henry David, *Civil Disobedience and Other Essays,* Prometheus Books, Amherst, NY, 1998.

Toms, Michael, "Money & Spirit: An Interview with Jacob Needleman," Program #2241, New Dimensions Radio, 1994.

Trent, Barbara (director), Barbara Trent, Joanne Doroshow, Nico Panigutti, and David Kasper (producers), *The Panama Deception,* Empowerment Project Production, 1992.

Walker, Brian (tr.), *Hua Hu Ching: The Teachings of Lao Tzu,* Clark City Press, 1992.

The Wall Street Journal Almanac 1998, Ballantine Books, New York, 1997.

White, John (ed.), *What is Enlightenment?,* "Meher Baba and the Quest of Consciousness" by Allan Y. Cohen, Paragon House, St. Paul, MN, 1995.

Winokur, Jon (ed.), *Zen To Go,* New American Library, New York, 1989.

Woodward, Bob, *The Choice: How Clinton Won,* Simon & Schuster, New York, 1996.

Wright, John W. (ed.), *The New York Times 1998 Almanac,* Penguin Reference, New York, 1997.

About the Author

ROBERT RABBIN is an author, speaker, and consultant. In 1969, he began to research mystic traditions and practice meditation and self-inquiry, continuing his studies for the next fifteen years while living throughout the United States, Europe, the Middle East, and India.

Since 1985, Robert has been lecturing and leading seminars, designing retreats for individuals, teams, and entire companies, and serving as an executive advisor to leaders from a broad range of companies and organizations.

Robert is the author of *The Sacred Hub: Living in Your Real Self* (1996), and co-author of *The Values Workbook: Creating Personal Truth at Work* (1997) and *Leadership in a New Era* (1994). He also wrote and produced a video about spirit in corporate America, *Brilliant Business: A Road Map to the 21st Century* (1997). He has published dozens of articles on the subjects of spirituality and leadership in magazines and journals, and has been a guest on numerous radio shows.

For contact information about the author, please visit his website at http://www.robrabbin.com.